Software Development
Targeted Applications

by D. James Benton
software available free online

Preface

In this text we will cover how to develop stand-alone applications specifically designed to perform one or more associated tasks. The term *software development* has been so diluted as to become meaningless. This same term should not be used to describe the process of creating a useful tool such as Microsoft® Excel® or composing three lines of python, yet so it is every day in countless posts on social media. We will demonstrate in this text what the term truly means and how to go about creating useful software tools. The obvious language for such is clearly C. The software described herein may be found free online at the link below and all will run on *any* version of Windows®.

https://www.dudleybenton.altervista.org/software/index.html

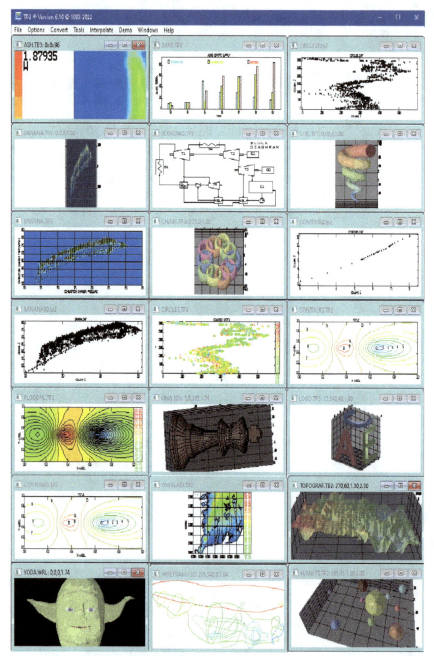

Figure 1. Multiple Document Interface (MDI)

Table of Contents   **page**

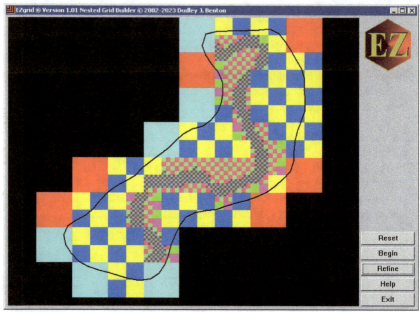

Figure 2. Interactive Grid Generator

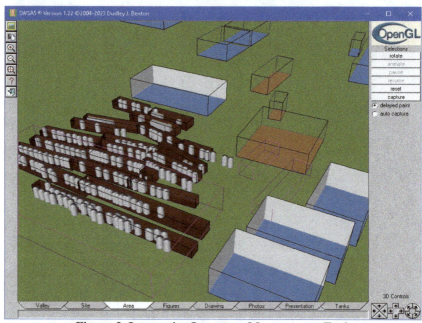

Figure 3. Interactive Inventory Management Tool

Chapter 1. What Is An Application?

A software application is a stand-alone program that performs a specific task or set of related tasks. A *stand-alone* program is an executable object that requires nothing beyond the operating system itself. An *executable* object is a collection of *machine* instructions, which tell the processor what to do. This differs considerably from *code* or *script*, which might provide information recognizable to a human. Of course, some humans (including this author) can read machine instructions. As these are *machine* instructions and not *code*, a compiler is required. A *compiler* reads code written by a human (or an AI) and converts this into the equivalent *machine instructions*. Most often when creating an executable, several pieces are brought together, which requires a linker. A *linker* brings together collections of *instructions* and *data* to form a complete *executable image*. Upon launch, the *executable image* is placed in memory and the processor is directed to perform the instructions contained therein. This is a multi-step process vastly more involved than simply composing three lines of python.

There are many operating systems but since the early days of digital computers, there have been *applications*. A compiler is an application and so is a linker. A code or text editing tool, such as Microsoft® notepad® is an application. If you were using the Windows® operating system and wanted to create a document, you would probably launch Word® to assist you in performing this task. If you wanted to create a spreadsheet, you would probably launch Excel®. If you wanted to create a presentation, you would probably launch PowerPoint®. While you may create many documents, spreadsheets, and presentations, you are not likely to have created Word®, Excel®, or PowerPoint®, as these *applications* were created by teams of developers working for Microsoft®.

You may need to purchase or create a custom application to perform some task that these others do not. For example, you may need to visualize three-dimensional data. No product sold by Microsoft® will perform such a task, but Tecplot™ will. You may need to plot meteorological data on a probability axis. Even Tecplot™ won't do this, but TP2[1] will. You might need to significantly modify an image. There are many tools to perform such tasks, including my personal favorite, Paint Shop Pro™. If you need to perform a unique task for which there is no "off the shelf" software available, you must then resort to *software development*.

All of the icons shown on the cover of this book, which is a screen capture from my laptop, represent individual stand-alone applications written specifically for the Windows® operating system, though each could be modified to run on some other operating system, such as LINUX. Something quite

---

[1] TP2 is the second-generation of TPLOT, which was developed by this author in 1980. The 'T' came from the original target device, a Tektronix 4010.

unusual about these 42 executables is that they will run on *any* version of Windows® from 95 to XP to Vista to 7 to 10 to 11 and beyond. This is intentional, as preserving investment in code and data is very important; therefore, I do not write code that will only work on one version or configuration of Windows® or in any way depends on third party support of any kind, as this would be irresponsible and foolish. This goal—software that will run on *any* version of Windows®—can easily be achieved following a simple set of guidelines.[2] These 42 icons represent only a few of the many such applications developed by this author over the past 50 years. Many of these programs and also some code may be found at the website listed beneath the Preface.

---

[2] For complete details see: *Version-Independent Programming: Code Development Guidelines for the Windows® Operating System*, by D. James Benton, ISBN-9781520339146, Amazon, 2016.

Chapter 2. Console Applications Can Be Very Useful

There are many different types of applications and also ways of categorizing these. Here we will separate applications by their interaction; that is, how the user goes about utilizing the tool. The first of these types goes all the way back to the earliest days of computers, before microchips to the days of mainframes. This is the way that DOS® worked before Windows®. There were no menus or buttons, let alone a mouse or touch screen. You simply *fed* data into the program and it *spit* out results. In the early days this involved a deck of cards or a reel of magnetic tape. There were even paper tapes with tiny punched holes. The mode of storage (cards, tape, or a digital file) is immaterial. What matters for our discussion here is that there is no interaction, only a fixed processing of information. This does not preclude *options*, as such could be provided as part of the input data; for example, we might want to curve-fit data using a first, second, third, or higher order. The desired order might be the first item input.

While a console application might seem like an archaic tool, this is not necessarily the case. What if you had to sort each file that came in over night by region and sales rep, sending copies to the individual sales rep, their supervisor, accounting, and the archives? What if there were hundreds? Wouldn't it be nice to dump these all into the digital equivalent of a sorting conveyor? What if every day you received a stack of text files containing a mixture of spaces or tabs and had to feed these into Excel? Wouldn't it be nice to have a simple program that read these files and wrote out comma-separated values that could be imported directly into Excel® with ease? I have just such a program called, txt2csv. It has saved me many hours of tedium.

Another example involving text files are those pesky ones from the few remaining people on the planet still using LINUX. I would get several of these a day from a coworker when I was working on a particular project. LINUX text files are problematic on any other operating system, including Windows® because each line of text is terminated with a linefeed (LF) character (ASCII 10). Lines of text in every other operating system are terminated with a pair of characters: a carriage return (CR) character (ASCII 13) and linefeed (LF). For this mind-numbing repetitive task, I wrote a little console application, lf2crlf, which accepts wild cards in the file name. Typing

```
lf2crlf *.txt
```

will fix every text file in the current folder, first checking to make sure it needs fixing.

What if you had to update every single one of 29,591 meteorological data files in the GSOD at NOAA's National Climate Data Center each day when the data came in? Wouldn't it be more convenient to create an application specifically designed to collect the data and put it in the proper files with no interaction on your part? This is what the folder on their ftp site looks like for just the year 2023 (each file is also compressed using UNIX gzip):

3

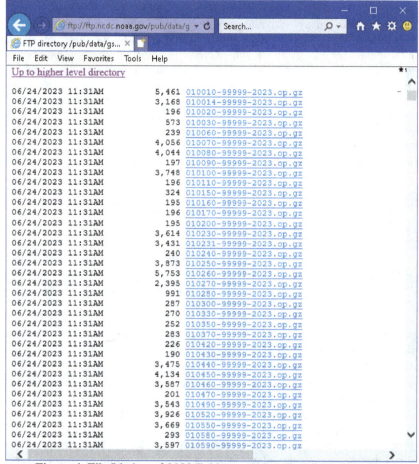

Figure 4. File Listing of 2023 Folder on NOAA's GSOD FTP Site

The simplest such program requires but a few lines of code plus that required to process the data. Having an entry point (declaring a function named, main) keys the compiler (Microsoft® Visual Studio® C) to create a console application. No special coding is necessary.

```
int main(int argc,char**argv,char**envp)
   {
   printf("begin console application\n");
   ReadData(argv[1]);
   ProcessData();
   WriteResults(argv[2]);
   return(0);
   }
```

This program (app1.c) can be found in the examples folder, which is available in the archive accompanying this text located at the web address listed beneath the Preface. The program is compiled using the following command:

```
cl /Ox /W3 /WX app1.c
```

The program is simply launched, passing it the name of the input and output files, as indicated below:

The arguments passed to function main are very important:

```
int main(int argc,char**argv,char**envp)
```

The first (argc) is the count or number of arguments. This is equal to one plus the number specified in the command launching the program. The first (or extra) argument is the name of the program, which you may find useful. The arguments (or passed parameters) are zero-terminated (that is C style) strings contained in the array of pointers, argv. These are zero references, as are all arrays in C. That is, the first argument is in argv[0], the second in argv[1], and so forth. The environment parameters are located in the array of zero-terminated strings in argument envp.

The environment parameters include the operating system version, the path, the user name, the processor type, etc. These depend on the version of Windows®, installed software, and user options. Environment parameters are often set in the System tab of the Control Panel. To display the environment parameters, open a command prompt and type: SET

Figure 5. Environment Parameters

As these environment parameters are readily available to your program, you can pass options to your programs by creating user variables in the environment. These can save time and be used to customize processing from one machine to another. You can also keep and modify options by placing them in some initialization file, for example: application.ini

I often use a little program that takes no input and has no menu but captures the entire screen every 100 msec (or 10 times per second) and saves this to sequentially numbered files capt0000.bmp, capt0001.bmp, etc. This facilitates the capture of videos that will play but won't let you save them. The main program is quite simple:

```
int WINAPI WinMain(HINSTANCE hCurrent,HINSTANCE
hPrevious,char*lCommand,int nShow)
{
MSG msg;
hInst=hCurrent;
RegisterClasses();
CreateWindows();
SetTimer(hMain,1,100,(TIMERPROC)Capture);
while(GetMessage(&msg,NULL,0,0))
   {
   TranslateMessage(&msg);
   DispatchMessage(&msg);
   }
return(0);
}
```

Unless the video captured fills the entire screen, it is necessary to crop each image to eliminate everything outside the desired area. This task is also accomplished by a console application in that it is not interactive and has no menu. The main program for this is also simple:

```
struct{int l,t,w,h;}crop={143,126,640,480};
int main(int argc,char**argv,char**envp)
{
char fname[32];
int h,i,j,w;
BITMAPINFOHEADER*b1,*b2;
DWORD rgb;
if(argc==5)
   {
   crop.l=atoi(argv[1]);
   crop.t=atoi(argv[2]);
   crop.w=atoi(argv[3]);
   crop.h=atoi(argv[4]);
   }
for(j=i=0;i<10000;i++)
   {
   sprintf(fname,"capt%04d.bmp",i);
   if(_access(fname,0))
```

6

```
    continue;
    printf("%s",fname);
    if((b1=BMPread(fname))==NULL)
    {
        printf("\ncan't read file\n");
        return(0);
    }
    if((b2=BMPresize(b1,crop.w,crop.h))==NULL)
    {
        printf("\ncan't duplicate image\n");
        return(0);
    }
    for(h=0;h<crop.h;h++)
    {
        for(w=0;w<crop.w;w++)
        {
            rgb=BMPGetPixel(b1,crop.l+w,b1->biHeight-crop.h-
crop.t+h);
            BMPput(b2,rgb,w,h);
        }
    }
    sprintf(fname,"CROP%04d.bmp",j++);
    printf(" %s\n",fname);
    if(BMPwrite(b2,fname))
    {
        printf("can't write cropped image\n");
        return(0);
    }
    free(b2);
    free(b1);
    }
    return(0);
}
```

The left, top, width, and height of the desired cropping area are passed as arguments, as in the following launch command:

```
crop 119 143 800 600
```

Default values are used if no arguments are specified. The processing is *hands free* and takes only seconds to process hundreds of frames.

More Examples of Hands-Free Processing

Windows® has the annoying habit of accumulating useless and unnecessary files in temporary folders. Unless you specifically delete these, they will continue to pile up forever, wasting disk space and in some cases exposing data to snooping. A simple program can be created and easily launched that will delete these *droppings*, again there is no need for user input and so interactive features are not needed for this application (cleantmp). The path to some of these turds can be found in the environment and there is a standard function to retrieve this information: GetEnvironmentVariable().

7

```
int main(int argc,char**argv,char**envp)
    {
    char path[FILENAME_MAX];
    RemoveFiles("C:\\TEMP");
    RemoveFiles("C:\\TMP");
    RemoveFiles("C:\\Windows\\TEMP");
    if(!GetEnvironmentVariable("USERPROFILE",path,
        sizeof(path)))
        return(0);
    if(path[strlen(path)-1]!='\\')
        strcat(path,"\\");
    if(_memicmp(path,"C:\\Documents and Settings",25)==0)
        strcat(path,"Application
        Data\\Microsoft\\Office\\Recent\\");
    else if(_memicmp(path,"C:\\Users",8)==0)

        strcat(path,"AppData\\Roaming\\Microsoft\\Office\\Rec
        ent\\");
    else
        return(0);
    RemoveFiles(path);
    return(0);
    }
```

Conversion of a text file to comma separated variables for easy import into Excel® is just one type of batch conversion that could save you a lot of time. I often work with geographical information and need this to be in a specific format: discrete polygons, as shown below:

```
POLY blue
482320.3 4442553.72
482327.1 4442562.58
482329.875 4442560.45
482323.025 4442551.55
482320.3 4442553.72
END
POLY red
482336.125 4442541.55
482342.975 4442550.45
482345.7 4442548.28
482338.9 4442539.42
482336.125 4442541.55
END
```

I often receive this data in some other format, including map points. While I could manipulate this information within Excel® to meet the project needs, this would be tedious indeed because Excel® does not recognize POLY or END as having any special significance and will not correctly draw polygons so defined. A conversion is therefore necessary. Some of these files contain many thousands of points, making *manual* conversion exceedingly tedious and wasteful. This is an excellent example of when a *hands-free* application is useful:

8

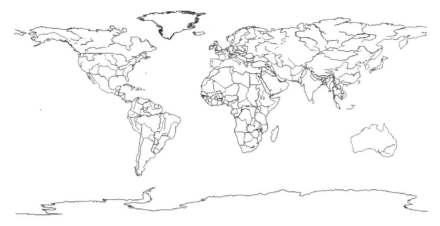

Figure 6. The World in Polygons

The following is a partial list of such *hands-free* applications that I wrotee and use on a routine basis:

3dsto3dv .... convert 3D Studio® file to finite elements
3dvtotri .... convert 3D Studio® file to triangles
3dvtowrl .... convert 3D Studio® file to Virtual Reality Markup format
amvac .... Automatic Multi-Variate Curve-Fitter
bifit .... binomial expansion curve-fitter
bin2dat........... convert a binary file to a single hexadecimal data statement
blokletr .... convert text to 8x8 block letters (also in text)
bmp2b............. convert Windows® bitmap image to black&white
bmp2gif .... convert one or more bitmaps to a single GIF
bmp2rm .... convert one or more bitmaps to a Raster MetaFile
bytedist........... display the distribution frequency of bytes in a file
chapter............ split a single text file into a separate text files by chapter
cleantmp .... delete clutter files from all temporary folders
clip2wmf .... copy image on clipboard to a Windows Meta-File
cmpcrop........... crop sequential images if they are significantly different
coefs .... coefficients for interpolating, integrating, or differentiating
colors.............. display current Windows® default colors
con2r.............. convert a 2D surface to contours, output polygons
crop................. crop sequential bitmaps (captured by scrncapt)
drives .... list details for all USB drives
elem3 .... convert closed polygons to triangular elements
emptydir .... list all empty folders on drive
encode .... encode a text string (convert to binary)
exe2scr............ convert an executable to a screen saver
extract............. extract (pick out and save) certain details from a webpage
fff.................... find all files

9

ffz	find all files plus look inside zip files too
fixhtml	remove Microsoft® trash from an html file
fixname	replace UNICODE with ASCII equivalent in file names
getdata	read binary output from VB and convert to ASCII
getpal	extract the palette from a bitmap
gettag	read the Dell service tag from current machine
gif2bmp	split a GIF into individual sequential bitmaps
gray2bw	convert gray image to black&white
initree	create a tree view representation of a C source file
lf2crlf	convert UNIX text file to Windows® format
lzari	compress one or more files using LZ-ARI algorithm
map2bin	convert a layered animation (MAP) file to sequential binary
map2bmp	convert a layered animation (MAP) file to sequential bitmaps
map2rm	convert a layered animation (MAP) file to Raster MetaFile
mzip	personalized modification of pkzip
orders	extract book orders from multiple spreadsheet files
polyf	fit a polynomial to a series of data
post	post-process model output (binary to text)
quotes	check for mismatched quotation marks in text
qwikpoly	quick polynomial curve fitter
range	read a data file and list lines, cols, min, and max
rank	convert Amazon book sales to rank
readtabl	read a GateCycle™ table file and output as text
rm2bmp	convert Raster MetaFile to sequential bitmaps
rm2gif	convert Raster MetaFile to GIF
scrncapt	capture screen 10 times per second, write as bitmaps
setftime	change the time stamp on a file
splitter	split a large file into a specified number of smaller files
splitwrl	split a Virtual Reality Markup file into individual polygons
tab2p2d	convert tab-delimited data to polygons
tritocsv	convert 3D triangles to comma-separated values for Excel®
txt2rtf	convert "decorated" text file to Rich Text Format
unspace	remove leading, trailing, and double spaces from text
usbvue	view contents of all USB drives
uts	UNICODE text search tool (findstr only work for ASCII)
walkdir	unpack all folders
words	find all words and list how many times they occur
wrlto3dv	convert Virtual Reality Markup file to generic 3D elements

All of these programs were written in C and compiled with Microsoft® Visual Studio®. For more on compilers see Appendix A.

Chapter 3. Classic (Minimalist) Menu-Driven Application

Menus have been around since the first version of the Windows® operating system. These are a familiar method of providing control and options to the user. One of the most common applications that has also been around since the beginning is notepad, the basic text editor, shown below open to a familiar text:

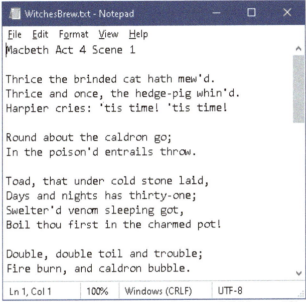

Figure 7. Classic Application (Microsoft® Notepad®)

The File menu pulls down to provide selections:

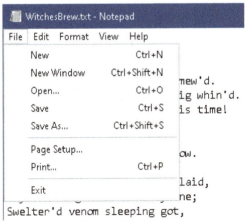

Figure 8. Classic Menu Drop-Down

There are two ways of building such a menu into a Windows® application: 1) repeatedly calling the AppendMenu() function or 2) defining the menu in a resource file and supplying this when the main window is created at launch time. The first option can be quite tedious but does allow for greater flexibility, especially if the menu changes depending on how the application is launched. The second option is much simpler and easy to implement. We will discuss both here.

Constructed Menu

We first consider a manually constructed menu of the first type. This is accomplished by calling a series of functions, which are described in the Win32 help as follows:

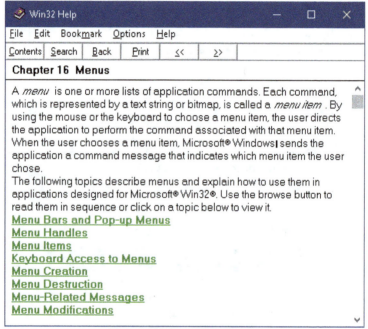

Figure 9. Menu Help Topics

In this section we are concerned with several of these subtopics, including: Menu Creation (a new menu), Menu Destruction (deleting an old menu), and Menu Modifications (used to build the new menu). There are two different functions used to create a classic menu or a popup one:

```
hm=CreateMenu();
hm=CreatePopupMenu();
```

After creating, we build the menu by repeatedly calling AppendMenu():

```
AppendMenu(hm,TRUE,PUSH_MIRROR   ,"mirror");
AppendMenu(hm,TRUE,PUSH_FLIP     ,"flip");
```

```
AppendMenu(hm,TRUE,PUSH_ROTATE90 ,"rotate 90°");
AppendMenu(hm,TRUE,PUSH_ROTATE180,"rotate 180°");
AppendMenu(hm,TRUE,PUSH_ROTATE270,"rotate 270°");
AppendMenu(hm,TRUE,PUSH_LARGER    ,"larger");
AppendMenu(hm,TRUE,PUSH_SMALLER   ,"smaller");
AppendMenu(hm,TRUE,PUSH_RESET     ,"reset");
```
passing the handle of the menu obtained at creation, the state (enabled or disabled), the ID, and description. The ID will be sent to the main procedure with a **WM_COMMAND**. The main procedure is defined when the class is registered, which begins receiving messages when the main window is created. Note that this is a Windows® *class* and has nothing whatsoever to do with C++ classes. The main class is defined and registered as follows:

```
void RegisterClasses()
  {
  WNDCLASS wc;
  wc.lpszwcName ="Application";
  wc.lpfnWndProc=(WNDPROC)MainProc;
  wc.hInstance  =hInstance;
  wc.hIcon      =LoadIcon(hInst,"MY_ICON");
  RegisterClass(&wc);
```

You must process these messages as illustrated below:

```
int WINAPI MainProc(HWND hWnd,UINT msg,WPARAM
  wParam,LONG lParam)
  {
  if(msg==WM_COMMAND&&wParam==MENU_ZOOM_IN)
    {
    ZoomIn();
    return(0);
    }
  if(msg==WM_COMMAND&&wParam==MENU_ZOOM_OUT)
    {
    ZoomOut();
    return(0);
    }
  return(DefWindowProc(hWnd,NULL,msg,wParam,lParam));
```

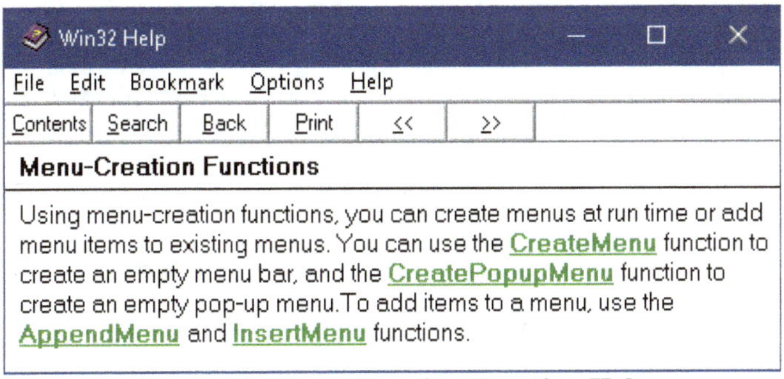

Figure 10. Menu Creation Function Help

13

The AppendMenu() function for instance, takes several parameters:

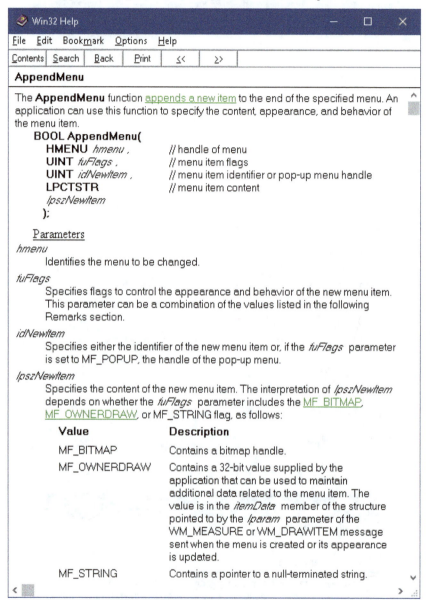

Figure 11. Details of AppendMenu() Function

While there is more flexibility with this method, it is more effort to program than the second menu option:

Resource Menus

The simplest way to create a classic menu is to define it in a resource (.RC) file, as illustrated below:

```
MENU MY_MENU
   BEGIN
      POPUP "File"
      BEGIN
         MENUITEM "Open",MENU_FILE_OPEN
         MENUITEM "eXit",MENU_FILE_EXIT
      END
      POPUP "Image"
      BEGIN
         MENUITEM "Enhance",MENU_DATA_ENHANCE
         MENUITEM "Reduce",MENU_DATA_REDUCE
         MENUITEM "Balance",MENU_DATA_BALANCE
         MENUITEM "Recolor",MENU_DATA_RECOLOR
         MENUITEM "Win16",MENU_DATA_WIN16
         MENUITEM "Win32",MENU_DATA_WIN32
         MENUITEM "Gray",MENU_DATA_GRAY
         MENUITEM "B&W",MENU_DATA_BLACK_AND_WHITE
      END
      POPUP "Data"
      BEGIN
         MENUITEM "Save",MENU_DATA_SAVE
         MENUITEM "Copy",MENU_DATA_COPY
      END
      POPUP "Help"
      BEGIN
         MENUITEM "Documentation",MENU_HELP_HOW2
         MENUITEM "About",MENU_HELP_ABOUT
      END
   END
```

Compile the resource with one simple command if using Visual Studio®:

```
rc /v myapp.rc
```

The compiled resource will be named myapp.res, which you link with the main program, also with one simple command:

```
cl /Ox /W3 /WX myapp.c myapp.res
```

Visual Studio® will compile and link with a single command. Some compilers require two separate steps. To use this menu within your program, first retrieve a handle to the menu from within the executable image (inside myapp.exe) by calling:

```
hm=LoadMenu(hInstance,"MY_MENU");
```

and then pass this handle when creating the main window, as shown below:

```
CreateWindow("MAIN","title",options,left,top,wide,
   high,NULL,hm,hInstance,NULL)
```

15

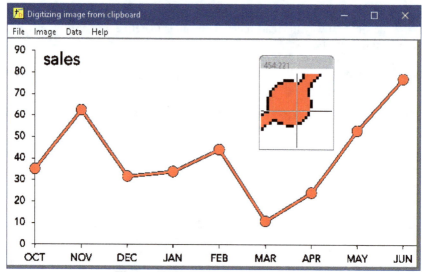
Figure 12. Example of Classic Menu

By default the menu will appear at the top of the main window beneath the caption bar with system menu (minimize, maximize, close [x]), if those options are specified at the time of creation. It is possible to move the menu to a different location by creating a child window, attaching the menu to the child window, and moving the child window to some other position within the main window, as shown below:

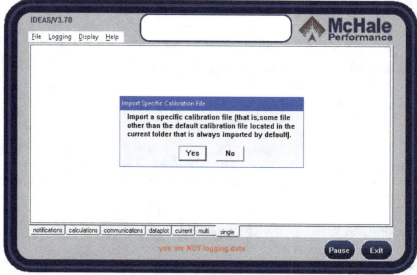
Figure 13. Example of Repositioned Menu

Chapter 4. Toolbar Menus

Toolbar menus appeared early on in Windows® and have been an important part of countless applications before the enormous (and useless) *ribbon bar* that consumes half your screen became popular with Microsoft® Office® 2007, which is a sad attempt to look more like an Apple® product. Ribbon bars take up lots of space and provide no useful functionality; therefore, we will not discuss how to create them here in this text. Simplicity and clarity are more appropriate goals to pursue in software development than frivolous decorations. Ironically, Steve Jobs stressed "how it works" over "how it looks"; though, as Bill Gates has clearly demonstrated, this doesn't necessarily translate into larger profits and market share.

Toolbar menus are easy to implement and can also be done two ways similar to that of the text menus (programmatically or using a resource). In either case, the basic building block is a bitmap mage having dimensions 16x16n where n is the number of buttons. Each button is 16x16 and are positioned beside each other without gaps. While it is possible to use up to 256 colors in such a toolbar, there is little point. Initially, only 16 were allowed. An example is shown below:

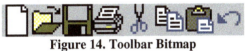

Figure 14. Toolbar Bitmap

These familiar shapes mean: new document, open document, save document, print document, cut, duplicate, paste, and undo. Countless such icons may be found online to use in your applications. In order to import such a toolbar as a resource without conversion, these must be stored as a BMP file with no compression. This is inserted in the resource (.RC) file as in:

```
ID_BITMAP BITMAP "TOOLBAR.BMP"
```

The toolbar is loaded and placed within the main window by calling the CreateToolbar() or CreateToolbarEx() function and passing certain parameters as detailed in the Win32 documentation:

```
hTool=CreateToolbarEx(hMain,
    WS_CHILD|WS_VISIBLE|TBSTYLE_TOOLTIPS,
    ID_TOOLBAR,sizeof(tbButton)/sizeof(tbButton[0]),
    hInstance,ID_BITMAP,
    tbButton,sizeof(tbButton)/sizeof(TBBUTTON),
    16,16,16,16,sizeof(TBBUTTON));
```

specifying the ID of the toolbar and bitmap plus a list of the commands, if you want to do this in a single step using the ...Ex() version of the library call, which is advisable. The other option is much more tedious, requiring a series of calls.

The list of commands can be a simple data statement:

```
TBBUTTON tbButton[]={
  {0,ID_NEW  ,TBSTATE_ENABLED,TBSTYLE_BUTTON,0,0},
  {1,ID_OPEN ,TBSTATE_ENABLED,TBSTYLE_BUTTON,0,0},
  {2,ID_SAVE ,TBSTATE_ENABLED,TBSTYLE_BUTTON,0,0},
  {3,ID_PRINT,TBSTATE_ENABLED,TBSTYLE_BUTTON,0,0},
  {4,ID_CUT  ,TBSTATE_ENABLED,TBSTYLE_BUTTON,0,0},
  {5,ID_COPY ,TBSTATE_ENABLED,TBSTYLE_BUTTON,0,0},
  {6,ID_PASTE,TBSTATE_ENABLED,TBSTYLE_BUTTON,0,0},
  {7,ID_UNDO ,TBSTATE_ENABLED,TBSTYLE_BUTTON,0,0}};
```

When the user clicks on any of the buttons, a WM_COMMAND message is sent to the main procedure where it can be processed. The result is shown in this next figure. Note that you can have a classic menu and also a toolbar menu. You can even assign the same ID to one member of each and process these as one.

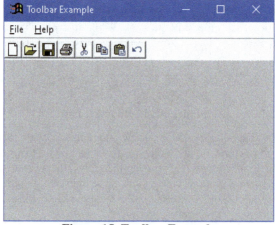

Figure 15. Toolbar Example

You can enhance a toolbar menu by adding *tips* that pop up when you hover over a button. This is done by adding a special handling sequence to the main procedure, as follows:

```
if(msg==WM_NOTIFY&&(HWND)lParam!=NULL)
  {
  LPTOOLTIPTEXT ttt;
  static char bufr[64];
  ttt=(LPTOOLTIPTEXT)lParam;
  if(ttt->hdr.code==TTN_NEEDTEXT)
    {
    LoadString(hInst,ttt->hdr.idFrom,bufr,
      sizeof(bufr));
    ttt->lpszText=bufr;
    SetWindowText(hMain,bufr);
    return(FALSE);
```

18

```
      }
   }
```

The menu commands are sent with identifier to the main procedure attached to WM_COMMAND and must be processed as before:

```
int WINAPI MainProc(HWND hWnd,UINT msg,WPARAM
   wParam,LONG lParam)
{
if(msg==WM_COMMAND&&wParam==ID_NEW)
   {
   CreateNewDocument();
   return(0);
   }
if(msg==WM_COMMAND&&wParam==ID_OPEN)
   {
   OpenExistingDocument();
   return(0);
   }
if(msg==WM_COMMAND&&wParam==ID_SAVE)
   {
   SaveDocument();
   return(0);
   }
   return(DefWindowProc(hWnd,NULL,msg,wParam,lParam));
}
```

Chapter 5. Button Options

Sometimes you may want more buttons than might fit on the toolbar. In that case, you can put them somewhere else on the main window, as illustrated in this next figure:

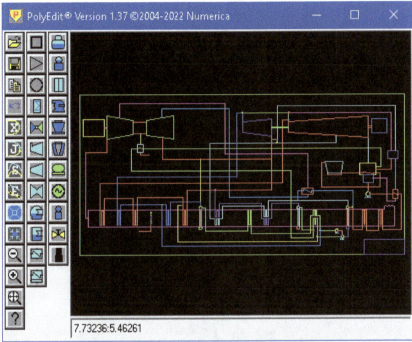

Figure 16. Example of Repositioned Buttons

The image on each button is still 16x16 only they are positioned along the left side of the main window. They could just as easily be placed on the right side or the bottom or both. It takes a little more effort to create this effect. While you could put all the buttons in a single row in a single bitmap file, they can be individual files. You could split bitmap up into pieces but this would take a few extra steps. List the button bitmaps in the resource file like this:

```
BOILER    BITMAP "..\\BOILER.BMP"
CHILL     BITMAP "..\\CHILL.BMP"
CIRCLE    BITMAP "..\\CIRCLE.BMP"
CLIP      BITMAP "..\\CLIP.BMP"
COND      BITMAP "..\\COND.BMP"
CT        BITMAP "..\\CT.BMP"
CTG       BITMAP "..\\CTG.BMP"
DEAER     BITMAP "..\\DEAER.BMP"
EVAP      BITMAP "..\\EVAP.BMP"
FWH       BITMAP "..\\FWH.BMP"
PUMP      BITMAP "..\\PUMP.BMP"
```

21

Before creating the main window, load all of the button bitmaps into memory (get the corresponding resources from the image), like this:

```
iBOILER=LoadBitmap(hInstance,BOILER);
iCHILL =LoadBitmap(hInstance,CHILL);
iCIRCLE=LoadBitmap(hInstance,CIRCLE);
iCLIP  =LoadBitmap(hInstance,CLIP);
iCOND  =LoadBitmap(hInstance,COND);
iCT    =LoadBitmap(hInstance,CT);
iCTG   =LoadBitmap(hInstance,CTG);
iDEAER =LoadBitmap(hInstance,DEAER);
iEVAP  =LoadBitmap(hInstance,EVAP);
iFWH   =LoadBitmap(hInstance,FWH);
iPUMP  =LoadBitmap(hInstance,PUMP);
```

You must also define a Windows® class with procedure to create the buttons and process related messages, including sending a command to the main procedure when a button is pushed. You must paint the bitmap into the client rectangle whenever the button procedure receives the WM_PAINT message. The button procedure might look like the following:

```
int WINAPI PushProc(HWND hWnd,DWORD msg,WPARAM
    wParam,LPARAM lParam)
{
if(msg==WM_CLOSE)
    return(FALSE);
if(msg==WM_CREATE)
    return(FALSE);
if(msg==WM_DESTROY)
    return(FALSE);
```

These first three messages are required to manage the button window.

```
if(msg==WM_LBUTTONDOWN)
    {
    if(GetWindID(hWnd)&0x20000)
        {
        SetWindID(hWnd,GetWindID(hWnd)|0x10000);
        InvalidateRect(hWnd,NULL,TRUE);
        }
    return(FALSE);
    }
if(msg==WM_LBUTTONUP)
    {
    if(GetWindID(hWnd)&0x20000)
        {
        SetWindID(hWnd,GetWindID(hWnd)&0x2FFFF);
        InvalidateRect(hWnd,NULL,TRUE);
        PostMessage(GetParent(hWnd),WM_COMMAND,
            MAKEDWORD(GetWindID(hWnd)&0xFFFF,BN_CLICKED),0);
        }
    return(FALSE);
    }
```

These next to messages fetch the window ID and convert it to a command.

```c
if(msg==WM_PAINT)
{
    int h,w;
    BITMAPINFOHEADER*bH;
    BITMAPINFO*bM;
    BYTE*bI;
    DWORD ROP;
    HDC hDC;
    PAINTSTRUCT pS;
    RECT rc;
    if((hDC=BeginPaint(hWnd,&pS))==NULL)
        Abort(__LINE__,"can't get device context\nerror
code %li",GetLastError());
    GetClientRect(hWnd,&rc);
    FrameRect(hDC,&rc,BlackBrush());
    rc.left  +=1;
    rc.right -=1;
    rc.top   +=1;
    rc.bottom-=1;
    if(GetWindID(hWnd)&0x10000)
        DrawEdge(hDC,&rc,EDGE_SUNKEN,BF_RECT);
    else
        DrawEdge(hDC,&rc,EDGE_RAISED,BF_RECT);
    rc.left  +=3;
    rc.right -=3;
    rc.top   +=3;
    rc.bottom-=3;
    bH=(BITMAPINFOHEADER*)GetUserData(hWnd);
    w=bH->biWidth;
    h=bH->biHeight;
    bM=(BITMAPINFO*)bH;
    bI=BMPimage(bH);
    if(GetWindID(hWnd)&0x20000)
        ROP=SRCCOPY;
    else
        ROP=NOTSRCCOPY;
    StretchDIBits(hDC,rc.left,rc.top,w,h,0,0,w,h,
        bI,bM,DIB_RGB_COLORS,ROP);
    EndPaint(hWnd,&pS);
    return(FALSE);
}
```

In order to make this look like a 3D button, you must adjust the edges, allowing ±3 pixels and utilizing the DrawEdge() library call, with flag depending on whether the button is out or pushed in. You can also change the appearance of the picture on the button using SRCCOPY or NOTSRCCOPY, which (as described in the Win32 help) paints the image or (logical) *not* (i.e., inverted colors).

23

```
    return(DefWindowProc(hWnd,msg,wParam,lParam));
    }
```
Always return with a call to the default window procedure to handle any messages that you don't specifically process. Before creating the main window, you must register the push button class:

```
WNDCLASS wc;
memset(&wc,0,sizeof(WNDCLASS));
wc.hInstance    =hInst;
wc.lpszClassName="PUSH";
wc.lpfnWndProc  =PushProc;
wc.hCursor      =LoadCursor(NULL,(char*)IDC_ARROW);
RegisterClass(&wc);
```

You must create each of the buttons *after* you create the main window, as these are separate windows and *children* of the main window.

```
#define CreateIconButton(ID,bI) CreateWindow("PUSH",\
    NULL,WS_CHILD|WS_CLIPSIBLINGS|WS_VISIBLE,\
    0,0,0,0,hMain,(void*)ID,hInst,NULL)
bBoiler=CreateIconButton(PUSH_BOILER,iBoiler);
bChill =CreateIconButton(PUSH_CHILL ,iChill );
bCircle=CreateIconButton(PUSH_CIRCLE,iCircle);
bCond  =CreateIconButton(PUSH_COND1 ,iCond  );
bCT    =CreateIconButton(PUSH_CT1    ,iCT    );
bCTG   =CreateIconButton(PUSH_CTG    ,iCTG   );
bDeaer =CreateIconButton(PUSH_DEAER ,iDeaer );
bEvap  =CreateIconButton(PUSH_EVAP  ,iEvap  );
bFWH   =CreateIconButton(PUSH_FWH1  ,iFWH   );
bPump  =CreateIconButton(PUSH_PUMP  ,iPump  );
```

You must position the buttons (of width w=h=16+8) within the client rectangle of the main window:

```
x=y=2;
MoveWindow(bBoiler,x,y,w,h,TRUE);y+=b;
MoveWindow(bCTG   ,x,y,w,h,TRUE);y+=b;
MoveWindow(bHPT   ,x,y,w,h,TRUE);y+=b;
MoveWindow(bIPT   ,x,y,w,h,TRUE);y+=b;
MoveWindow(bLPT   ,x,y,w,h,TRUE);y+=b;
MoveWindow(bCond  ,x,y,w,h,TRUE);y+=b;
MoveWindow(bFWH   ,x,y,w,h,TRUE);y+=b;
MoveWindow(bPUMP  ,x,y,w,h,TRUE);y+=b;
```

The "y+=b;" on the end of each line positions the next button 24 pixels below the previous one.

Larger Buttons

Sometimes you may want bigger buttons with more detailed pictures on them. These don't provide additional function but can change the appearance of the application. Buttons can also change the shape of the user area as presented on the screen. This next figure illustrates larger buttons with more colors (up to 2^{24} possible):

24

Figure 17. Application with Large Repositioned Buttons

Programmatically, this look is achieved with the same code as for the smaller repositioned buttons, only using larger bitmaps shifted to the right side of the main window.

Non-Rectangular Buttons

We have already seen non-rectangular buttons in Figure 13. A closer look:

Figure 18. Close Up of Non-Rectangular Buttons

The question remains: how to draw them. First, we will need a separate bitmap image for each state, which will be painted accordingly:

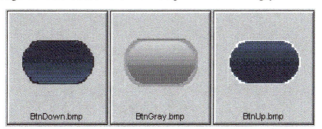

Figure 19. Separate Bitmap for Each Button State

25

We paint (draw) the text (Pause or Exit) after drawing the button using a color as appropriate (white, black, gray).

```
SetTextColor(hDC,0xFFFFFF);
SetTextColor(hDC,0x9F9F9F);
SetTextColor(hDC,0x404040);
```

and can even add a staggered line of text to make a 3D appearance:

```
GetTextExtentPoint32(hDC,text,i,&st);
TextOut(hDC,(rc.right-st.cx)/2,rc.bottom/2
    -st.cy,text,i);
GetTextExtentPoint32(hDC,text+i+1,l-i-1,&st);
TextOut(hDC,(rc.right-st.cx)/2,rc.bottom/2,
    text+i+1,l-i-1);
```

Chapter 6. Main Window Options

There are three main types of main windows supported by the Microsoft® Windows® operating system: 1) fixed-size with single or floating child windows, 2) adjustable-size with single or floating child windows, and 3) one main window with any number of child windows arranged in specific ways. This last type is called a Multiple Document Interface or MDI. These three types correspond to specific options or creation statements, namely the following:

```
hMain=CreateWindowEx(WS_EX_DLGMODALFRAME|
   WS_EX_TOPMOST,"MAIN","title",
   WS_POPUPWINDOW|WS_CAPTION|WS_VISIBLE,
   left,top,wide,high,
   NULL,NULL,hInst,NULL);
hMain=CreateWindow("MAIN",title,
   WS_OVERLAPPEDWINDOW|WS_VISIBLE,
   left,top,wide,high,
   NULL,NULL,hInst,NULL);
hMain=CreateWindow("MAIN","title",
   WS_OVERLAPPEDWINDOW|WS_CLIPCHILDREN|WS_VISIBLE,
   left,top,wide,high,
   NULL,NULL,hInst,NULL);
hClnt=CreateWindow("MDICLIENT",NULL,
   WS_CHILD|WS_VISIBLE|WS_CLIPSIBLINGS|
   WS_CLIPCHILDREN,
   left,top,wide,high,
   hMain,NULL,hInst, &ccs);
```

Note the first case uses CreateWindowEx() while the rest CreateWindowEx(). This allows passing the window style option specifying this to be a dialog modal frame, WS_EX_DLGMODALFRAME. Note that the third case (i.e., the MDI) must also create the child windows, which are called MDI clients (defined by the class name "MDICLIENT") and are thus handled by the procedure already in the library and not unique to this program. Note also the necessity of setting options to handle one child possibly obscuring another with the window style WS_CLIPCHILDREN and WS_CLIPSIBLINGS.

We saw an example of a rigid frame main window in Figure 13 and also Figure 17. We will discuss how to create the custom frame in Figure 13 later in this chapter. We saw an example of the second type (adjustable frame) main window in Figure 16. Figure 1 shows a MDI application with 21 children. Most users of the Windows® operating system are familiar with all three types and the menu options for arranging the MDI children: tile and cascade. This operation (arranging the child windows) is accomplished by the procedure in the library and does not require a user-defined procedure.

27

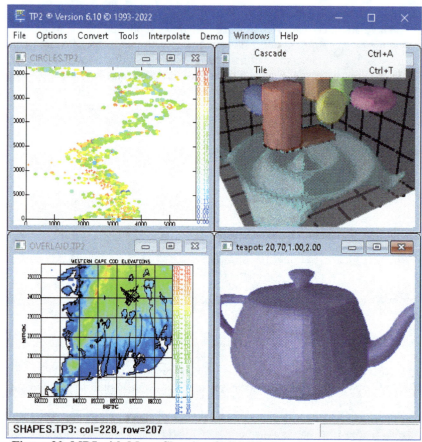

Figure 20. MDI with Menu Showing Child Window Arrangement Options

Adjustable-size windows (main and child) can be stretched with the mouse. Windows which can accept such modifications will display a diagonal two-pointed arrow when the mouse hovers over a corner, as shown in the lower right corner of this next figure:

Figure 21. Adjustable-Size Main Window

If the window can't be resized (option WS_EX_DLGMODALFRAME), the diagonal arrow will not appear (designated type 1 in this chapter). MDI windows will automatically resize using the built-in procedure without relying on a user-defined procedure (designated type 3 in this chapter). The second type of window (adjustable but neither Dialog Modal Frame nor MDI) rely on the user to make the necessary adjustments in response to the WM_SIZE message, which will be passed to the main window or the child window, depending on the focus. When processing this message, you can optionally check for resizing or restoring or neither, using some combination or flag to specify a default resizing of the windows. If so specified, the indicated new size is passed as a double word (unsigned 32-bit value) with the width in the low portion and the height in the high portion:

```
if(msg==WM_SIZE)
  {
  if(wParam==SIZE_MAXIMIZED||wParam==SIZE_RESTORED)
    PositionWindows(LOWORD(lParam),HIWORD(lParam));
  else
    PositionWindows(0,0);
  return(FALSE);
  }
```

If you don't want the window to be resized, you can elect to not process this message by simply returning a zero:

```
if(msg==WM_SIZE)
  return(FALSE);
```

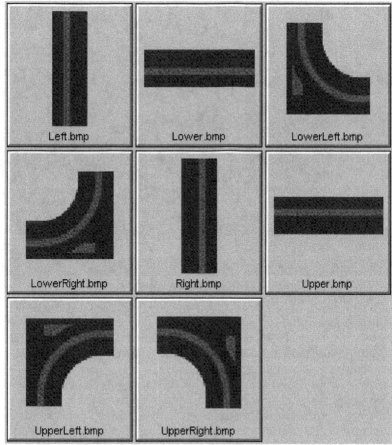

Figure 22. Corner and Edge Pieces as Bitmaps

Non-Rectangular or Custom Edge Windows

Figure 13 shows a window that is not rectangular and has a custom edge. Intercepting the corresponding messages will make this an owner-drawn window. To accomplish this we need the whole window or the corners and sides as bitmaps, which we put in the resource file and load before creating the main window as before with the button images, as shown at the bottom of the previous page. We first fill the window with the background color (LTGRAY) and then paint the corners and sides:

```
if(msg==WM_PAINT)
{
HDC hDC;
PAINTSTRUCT ps;
RECT rc;
hDC=BeginPaint(hWnd,&ps);
GetClientRect(hWnd,&rc);
FillRect(hDC,&rc,GetStockObject(LTGRAY_BRUSH));
PaintBitmap(hDC,Rect(0,0,bUpperLeft->biWidth,
  bUpperLeft->biHeight),bUpperLeft,0);
PaintBitmap(hDC,Rect(rc.right-bUpperRight->biWidth,
  0,rc.right,bUpperRight->biHeight),bUpperRight,0);
PaintBitmap(hDC,Rect(0,rc.bottom-
  bLowerLeft->biHeight,bLowerLeft->biWidth,
  rc.bottom),bLowerLeft,0);
PaintBitmap(hDC,Rect(rc.right-
  bLowerRight->biWidth,rc.bottom-
  bLowerRight>biHeight,rc.right,
  rc.bottom),bLowerRight,0);
PaintBitmap(hDC,Rect(bUpperLeft->biWidth,0,
  rc.right-bUpperRight->biWidth,
  bUpper->biHeight),bUpper,1);
PaintBitmap(hDC,Rect(bLowerLeft->biWidth,
  rc.bottom-bLower->biHeight,rc.right-
  bUpperRight->biWidth,rc.bottom),bLower,1);
PaintBitmap(hDC,Rect(0,bUpperLeft->biHeight,
  bLeft->biWidth,rc.bottom-
  bLowerLeft->biHeight),bLeft,1);
PaintBitmap(hDC,Rect(rc.right-bRight->biWidth,
  bUpperRight->biHeight,rc.right,
  rc.bottom-bLowerRight->biHeight),bRight,1);
return(FALSE);
}
```

These steps alone would still result in a rectangular window. In order to give this window a truly oval shape, we must somehow prevent painting of the frame in the corners. What makes this task more interesting is that we want a particular shape that is not often associated with applications, at least not in the Windows® operating system. To accomplish this, we utilize two built-in functions that have been included in Windows® from the beginning, although

31

few programmers know about it. These are *clipping regions* and *rounded rectangles*, both native Windows® objects. We can use this same user-defined function as a shell to apply this effect to one or more main or child windows:

```
void SetClipRgn(int w,int h,int r)
{
static HRGN hClip;
if(hClip)
  {
  SetWindowRgn(hMain,NULL,FALSE);
  DeleteObject(hClip);
  }
hClip=CreateRoundRectRgn(0,0,w,h,r,r);
SetWindowRgn(hMain,hClip,FALSE);
RedrawWindow(GetDesktopWindow(),NULL,NULL,
  RDW_ALLCHILDREN|RDW_ERASE|RDW_ERASENOW|
  RDW_INTERNALPAINT|RDW_INVALIDATE|RDW_UPDATENOW);
}
```

where *w* and *h* are the overall width and height, respectively, and *r* is the radius of the arc. Notice the `static HRGN hClip` above. If the function has already been called, this will not be NULL and we will simply implement the same as before and return. If the function hasn't been called before (i.e., first time in), we create the rounded rectangular region then set (apply) the region to the handle of the main window (hMain) and redraw, which will send a WM_PAINT message back to the main procedure where it will be processed and all the parts of the window will be painted again, only this time the painting will be limited to inside the clipping region.

Chapter 7. Command Line Arguments

We have already seen in Chapter 2 how command line arguments are passed to a console application and how this can be a convenient time saver. This same functionality can be built into a Graphical User Interface (GUI) or any interactive application. The launch command is the same but the implementation is slightly different. These same parameters (argument count, array of pointers to arguments, and array of pointers to environment parameters) that are passed in the main function call:

```
int main(int argc,char**argv,char**envp)
```

are available in global memory locations, outside the main program but inside the memory space containing and belonging to the executable. These are only slightly different:

```
extern int __argc;
extern char**__argv;
extern char**_environ;
```

These three (and the previous) are prepared by the operating system during the launch process. The actual (original, unprocessed) command line is not broken up into individual arguments separated by a comma or other delimiter. It is just a single string in a buffer of fixed length. The splitting and zero-delimiting is all done by the operating system before jumping to the main procedure. This is actually a hold-over from DOS®, where this information was part of the executable header, also in a fixed location and of fixed size.

The main procedure in a Windows® console application is main() and in an interactive one is WinMain(). These names are not optional and only one may appear in an application. Anything else will result in a compiler and/or linker error. There are many situations when you might want to specify a file and/or option for an interactive application upon launch. My digitizing program (Figure 12) is one example. If you supply the name of an image file to be digitized at launch time, it will be opened automatically. If not and there is an image on the clipboard at the time of launch, this will be loaded automatically. If neither of these is the case, you can open a file using the classic menu.

The following is an example of processing optional arguments within an interactive application, which must appear within WinMain() before or after creation of the windows but before the main message loop:

```
for(i=1;i<__argc;i++)
    {
    if(!stricmp(__argv[i],"-AUTO"))
        auto_capture=2;
    else if(!stricmp(__argv[i],"-MAP2BMP"))
        map2bmp=-1;
    else if(!stricmp(__argv[i],"-BACK"))
        back_light=1;
    else if(!stricmp(__argv[i],"-BLEN"))
        flat_surf=1;
```

33

```
else if(!stricmp(__argv[i],"-CYCLE"))
   plot_loop=-2;
else if(!stricmp(__argv[i],"-EXPAND"))
   expand=TRUE;
else if(!stricmp(__argv[i],"-FILL"))
   polyfill=TRUE;
else if(!stricmp(__argv[i],"-FLAT"))
   flat_surf=-1;
}
```

The main message loop will look like this:

```
while(GetMessage(&msg,NULL,0,0))
   if(!TranslateAccelerator(hMain,hAcc,&msg))
      if(!TranslateMessage(&msg))
         DispatchMessage(&msg);
```

The handle to the table of keyboard accelerators is hAcc, which will be discussed in the next chapter. If we translate the message (perform any modifications and identify which window the message is intended for) and the TranslateMessage() function returns TRUE, it has already been sent to a different window. If not, then we send it to the appropriate window by passing it to DispatchMessage().

Chapter 8. Keyboard Accelerators

Keyboard accelerators in an interactive Windows® application are user-defined keystrokes that generate a WM_COMMAND message, which is sent to the main procedure through the main message loop. At the end of the previous chapter we had the following instruction inside the loop:

```
if(!TranslateAccelerator(...
```

If the message is a keyboard accelerator, then this procedure will return TRUE and the message should not be processed because it has already been converted into a WM_COMMAND message. The easiest way to define a list of keyboard accelerators is to put them in a resource file, as in:

```
FAST ACCELERATORS
   BEGIN
      VK_F1   ,PUSH_HELP ,VIRTKEY
      VK_HOME,PUSH_HOME  ,VIRTKEY
      VK_PGUP,PUSH_PGUP  ,VIRTKEY
      VK_PGDN,PUSH_PGDN  ,VIRTKEY
      VK_END ,PUSH_END   ,VIRTKEY
      VK_F4   ,PUSH_QUIT ,VIRTKEY,ALT
   END
```

Pressing the F1 key will send the a WM_COMMAND message with the parameter PUSH_HELP, which must be defined in a list elsewhere, such as:

```
enum{PUSH_HELP=0x0F00,PUSH_HOME,PUSH_PGUP,PUSH_PGDN,
   PUSH_END,PUSH_QUIT};
```

Before entering the main message loop, you must get a handle to the accelerator list by calling the LoadAccelerators() function:

```
hAcc=LoadAccelerators(hInst,"FAST");
```

Features can be added in this way to enhance the user's experience.

Chapter 9. Interactive and/or Console Applications

It is possible to create a single application that will be interactive (i.e., a GUI) and also non-interactive (hands-free batch processing). Why would anyone want to do such a thing? Flexibility Plus Continuity: A tool that works either way and only one thing to validate. But the compiler and/or linker will fuss if you have a main() and also a WinMain(). Right, but we don't need both to have the functionality, only to have that functionality without any additional effort. We must have WinMain() else many essential element of the Windows® user interface library will not be available at runtime. We can create a console the same way main() does, only explicitly rather than implicitly.

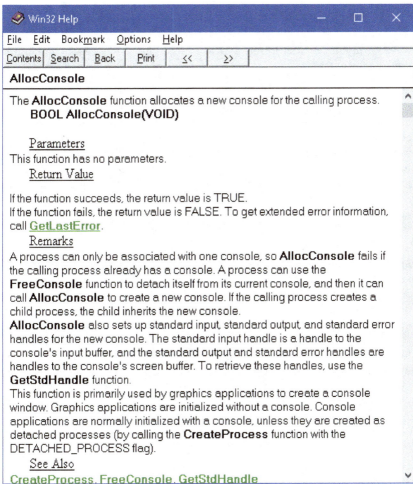

Figure 23. Win32® Help for AllocConsole()

This is how we create the console from inside WinMain():

```
AllocConsole();
CenterWindowOnScreen(GetConsoleWindow());
BringWindowToTop(GetConsoleWindow());
stdInput=GetStdHandle(STD_INPUT_HANDLE);
stdOutput=GetStdHandle(STD_OUTPUT_HANDLE);
```

We allocate (create) the console, center it on the screen, bring it to the top, and get a handle to the standard input and output streams. These handles can be used to read any data "piped" into the process with the less than (<) sign and write any output to the console. We write to the console using:

```
WriteConsole(stdOutput,bufr,1,&1,NULL);
```

We can simply close the console

```
FreeConsole();
```

when we're done or wait for the user to indicate that they are ready to close by pressing the Enter key.

Examples of Dual-Purpose Applications

I have developed more than two-dozen such dual-purpose applications. The first group of these began as non-interactive programs before Microsoft® created Windows® or I ever had a microprocessor or laptop. These programs were developed to analyze the thermal cycle plus environmental discharge and impact of power plants. Initially, only two nuclear plants were modeled but this later grew to nine nuclear plants and twelve coal-fired ones. The codes originally ran on an IBM and later CDC mainframe, then on an HP-1000 minicomputer, and finally on a PC, which was at first only DOS® but later Windows®. All of these codes now run on Windows 11.

The original flow of data was to read operational settings from an initialization file or option switches plus environmental data from magnetic tapes. Eventually, all of the input was gathered from digital text files, which is how they currently function. The input was data and so was the output (data in the form of calculation results). If graphs of the various internal functions were needed, say for the purposes of illustration or validation, this originally required code modification and recompiling. With the conversion to interactive functionality on the Windows® operating system, this became just another option; hence, the dual-purpose: launch the executable with a data file and pipe (i.e., redirect with the greater than (>) sign) to a file or launch the executable and pick which graphic to generate and display.

Consider one of these dual-mode applications written to model the thermal cycle at TVA's Watts Bar Nuclear Plant. The batch input in this case consists of dry-bulb and wet-bulb temperatures and looks like this:

```
39,37
38,35
37,33
36,32
```

```
35,32
34,30
33,30
32,29
33,30
32,29
33,30
34,31
35,32
37,33
38,34
40,35
42,36
39,33
39,33
37,32
. . .
```

The program is launched and passed the name of the file, which produces the following output:

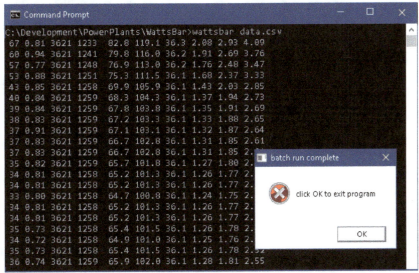

Figure 24. Batch Output of Watts Bar Model

The calculations require a collection of models: the reactor, steam system, condenser, pumps, and cooling towers. Some of these are basic thermodynamic models while others, such as the cooling tower calculations, which are implemented as curve-fits of a more detailed combined heat and mass transfer model (FACTS) plus information provided by the manufacturer (Research-Cottrell). The calculations are also based on performance curves provided by the steam turbine manufacturer (Westinghouse) and the condenser manufacturer.

Figure 25. Watts Bar User Interface

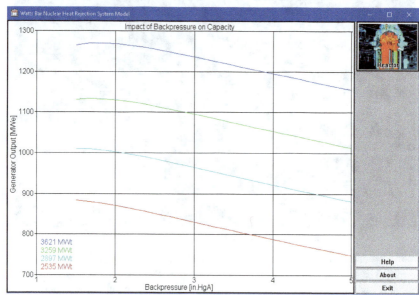

Figure 26. WBN Steam Generator Curves

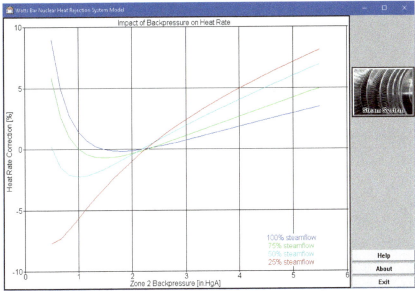

Figure 27. WBN Steam Turbine Backpressure Curves

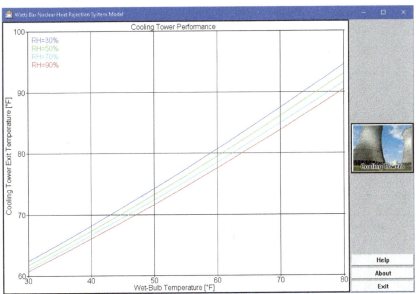

Figure 28. WBN Cooling Tower Curves

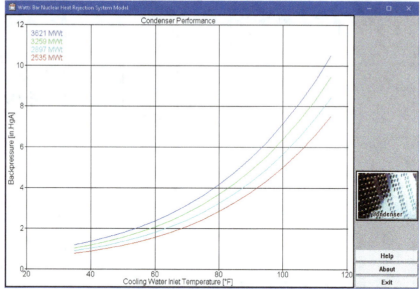

Figure 29. WBN Condenser Curves

How we produce these graphs will be covered in the next chapter, suffice it to say that such capability is an important part of many applications.

<u>Other Advantages to Batch Processing</u>

There are other advantages or uses for a software tool that can be utilized without requiring direct user input; that is, hands-free operation, such as we have seen with this Watts Bar Nuclear Plant model. You might want to use the program interactively for a variety of tasks or perhaps use it inside some other program so as to access features not available otherwise and without excessive duplication of efforts.

One such program that I utilize in this way is CREST, which solves chemical reactions. You provide it with a property database, a reaction (that is, a list of reactants and their molar quantities), plus the conditions (temperature, pressure) and optional constraints (constant pressure, constant temperature, set or zero heat transfer), and it calculates the products (molecular outcome of the reaction). A typical reaction might be the combustion of methane (CH_4) with oxygen (O_2).

```
!Methane+2.5Odia=!H+Hdia+O+Odia+Water
  +Hydroxl+C+Cmonox+Cdiox
```

The most unique thing about CREST is that it can handle *real* (as opposed to *ideal*) properties of the reactants and products. Any molecule name followed by an exclamation point (!) will be treated as *real* (the default behavior is *ideal*). If the exclamation point precedes all of the reactants (on the left side of the equals =) then all of those molecules are treated as *real*.

42

CREST will solve the reaction at one condition or you can select from sever choices to solve over a range of temperatures or pressures or even vary the number of moles of one of the reactants. The user interface looks like this:

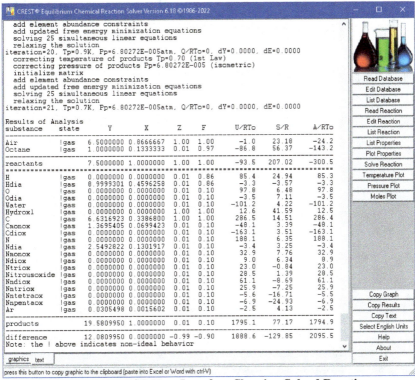

Figure 30. CREST User Interface Showing Solved Reaction

CREST can solve a reaction over a range of conditions and can display the results graphically using the same code that I developed to plot the curves in the Watts Bar model. We see those graphical results in this next figure:

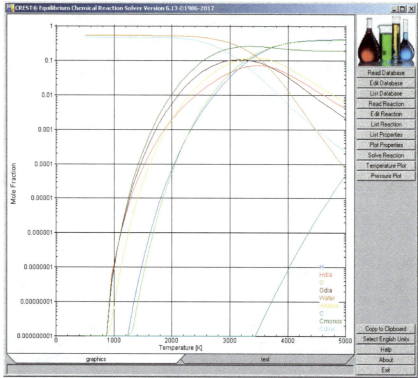

Figure 31. CREST Chemical Reaction Curves

Having validated CREST, we might want to use it inside some other program to solve a chemical reaction. This is easily accomplished because it has this same built-in functionality of operating interactively or in hands-free batch mode by simply launching it and passing two input files (database plus reaction) and one or more options to pick the constraints. This isn't just a convenience. There are some things that CREST isn't set up to do, including calculating the inputs given desired output, whether these be mole fractions or temperatures or pressures.

Sometime we have an outcome and must solve an implicit problem. We can accomplish this by creating a wrapper or shell that feeds the problem into CREST, reads the results, adjusts the inputs, runs it again, checks the results again, and so forth until we obtain the desired outcome. The steps and necessary code are simple:

1) guess inputs
2) create input file
3) run program
4) get results (read output)
5) compare outcome to target, if close enough quit
6) adjust inputs
7) return to 2)

For CREST this looks like:

Figure 32. CREST Running in Batch Mode

Chapter 10. Draw Your Own Graphs

We have already seen graphs similar to what you might create with Excel® only inside some other application in Figures 26, 27, 28, 29, and 31. Graphs like these are quite helpful and important but how do we create them?

I can't stress strongly enough what an *extremely bad* decision a programmer makes by utilizing some third party code in their own work. The most egregious form of this is called Object Linking and Embedding, or OLE. Never under any circumstances use OLE for any reason! You *will* regret it. Something will change, Microsoft® will update Windows®, and your application will *stop working*. You will have no way of fixing it because you have *no control* over the third party (who may have died in the meanwhile) on whose work you have foolishly come to depend. For more on this, see my book, *Version-Independent Programming*.

With this said, we come to the matter of how to draw a graph. TPLOT (and later TP2) was one of the first very large programs I wrote. This was out of necessity in order to create technical graphics for my dissertation in 1980. There were no such programs available for sale at that time so buying one wasn't an option. As they say, "necessity is the mother of invention," and so it was with TPLOT.

When you get down to it, the task is not that difficult: you draw the axes, put the numbers along the bottom and up the side, then draw the data. It's all a bunch of lines, even the lettering. You can use Windows® functions, such as TextOut(), or you can simply draw the letters. Back in 1980 I had to create my own letters because Windows® didn't come out until 1985. Needless to say, this took a lot of work. Each character consists of one or more strokes so there must be some way of starting and stopping the strokes and also ending the character. There are 256 characters in the complete ASCII set, which I wanted to have available. There are times when you want thin and also bold characters so that at least two sets are required. Since we're drawing graphs, we will also need symbols like: circle, triangle, diamond, etc. We might also want Greek letters. I have been using this same set for 43 years:

```
short norm_set[]={
/* A033 */  1610,  1436,  1836,  1610,-1504,  1102,  1500,
   2002,  1504,    0,
/* A034 */   140,   127,-2240,  2227,    0,
/* A035 */  1540,   300,-2640,  1400,  -324,  2824,  -113,
   2613,    0,
/* A036 */  1040,   994,-1840,  1794,-2729,  2332,  1834,
   1034,   532,   129,
             126,   322,   521,   819,  2016,  2314,  2513,
   2710,  2705,  2302,
            1800,  1000,   502,   105,    0,
```

```
/* A037 */  2840,   100,  -840, 1136, 1132, 1029,   727,
   427,   130,   134,
              238,   540,   840, 1138, 1636, 2036, 2538,
  2840,-2213, 1911,
             1708, 1704, 2000, 2300, 2602, 2806, 2809,
  2513, 2213,    0,
/* A038 */  3023, 3025, 2827, 2727, 2525, 2421, 2111,
  1806, 1502, 1200,
              700,   402,   204,   108,   111,   215,   417,
  1425, 1527, 1730,
             1734, 1538, 1240, 1038,   834,   830, 1025,
  1219, 2006, 2202,
             2500, 2800, 3002, 3004,     0,
```

This is what they look like rendered as strokes:

Figure 33. TPLOT/TP2 Stroke Characters

48

This reusable code should be written so as to provide flexibility. This is what it looks like with linear axes:

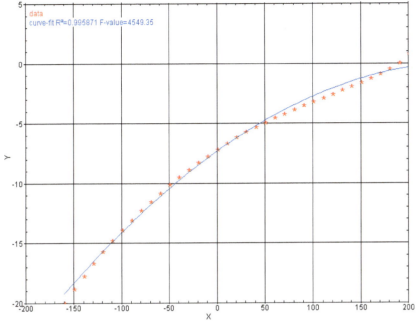

Figure 34. Linear Axes

Logarithmic axes are often required and so this capability must also be built into the code:

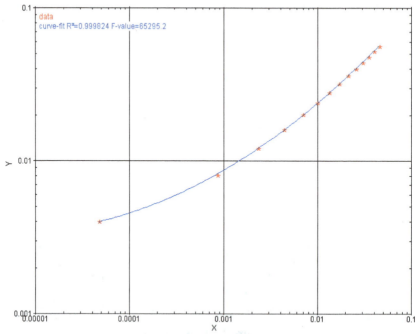

Figure 35. Log-Log Axes

Another useful axis is probability. Excel® and, in fact, no Microsoft® product can handle a probability axis, yet these have been used for many decades and were once available on printed sheets. As detailed in my book, *Forecasting*, probability axes are often used to plot historical occurrence, such as floods and storms. The axis looks like this when wrapped back on itself:

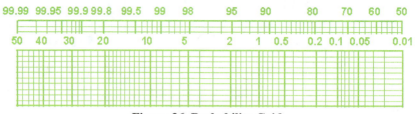

Figure 36. Probability Grid

The important thing about this particular grid (i.e., probability axis) is that the familiar bell-shaped curve, which often appears in statistical analyses, when integrated to become the *cumulative probability* displays as a *straight line*. This facilitates extending it out on either end, which is where we get the prediction of a 100-year and 500-year flood from when only 75 years of historical data are available. Here we see data plotted on just such a graph with a probability axis:

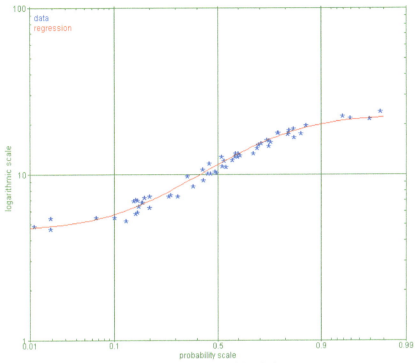

Figure 37. Probability Axis

Here we see the axes drawn and also data points (blue *) plus a red curve. Some sort of legend is also to be expected and the option of moving this to any one of the four corners is a useful functionality too. A snippet of the code to draw the axis is shown here:

```
for(X=Xm;;X+=dX)
    {
    AxisNumber(Xaxis,Xm,Xx,X);
    x=nint(Bx+Ax*X);
    sText=GetTextSize(hDC,bufr);
    TextOut(hDC,x-sText.cx/2,rp.bottom+sTick.cx/4,bufr,
        (int)strlen(bufr));
    DrawLine(hDC,x,rp.bottom+sTick.cx/4,x,
        rp.top-sTick.cx/2);
    if(X+dX>Xx+dX/10)
        break;
    if(Xaxis==LOGARITHMIC)
        {
        for(k=2;k<=9;k++)
```

51

```
      {
      x=nint(Bx+Ax*(X+log10(k)));
      DrawLine(hDC,x,rp.bottom-sTick.cx/2
        x,rp.bottom);
      DrawLine(hDC,x,rp.top,x,rp.top+sTick.cx/2);
      }
    }
```

This is a snippet of the code that draws the data:

```
  for(s=i=0;s<sets;s++)
    {
    SetTextColor(hDC,Color[s]);
    hPen=SelectObject(hDC,hPen);
    DeleteObject(hPen);
    hPen=CreatePen(PS_SOLID,1,Color[s]);
    hPen=SelectObject(hDC,hPen);
    hBrush=SelectObject(hDC,hBrush);
    DeleteObject(hBrush);
    hBrush=CreateSolidBrush(Color[s]);
    hBrush=SelectObject(hDC,hBrush);
    if(type[s]==POLYGON)
      {
      POINT*Pt;
      Pt=allocate(__LINE__,abs(points[s]),
        sizeof(POINT));
      for(p=0;p<abs(points[s]);p++,i++)
        {
        Pt[p].x=nint(Bx+Ax*Xp[i]);
        Pt[p].y=nint(By-Ay*Yp[i]);
        }
      Polygon(hDC,Pt,abs(points[s]));
      release(__LINE__,Pt);
      }
    else if(type[s]==SYMBOL)
      {
      for(p=0;p<abs(points[s]);p++,i++)
        {
        x=nint(Bx+Ax*Xp[i]);
        y=nint(By-Ay*Yp[i]);
        DrawSymbol(hDC,'*',x,y);
        }
      }
    else
      {
      x2=nint(Bx+Ax*Xp[i]);
      y2=nint(By-Ay*Yp[i]);
      for(p=1,++i;p<abs(points[s]);p++,i++)
        {
        x1=x2;
        y1=y2;
```

```
        x2=nint(Bx+Ax*Xp[i]);
        y2=nint(By-Ay*Yp[i]);
        DrawLine(hDC,x1,y1,x2,y2);
        }
    }
}
```

The entire code (plots.c and plots.h) can be found within several of the archives located at the webpage listed beneath the Preface. It isn't all that complicated and burdensome and certainly not worth the hassle of using OLE. One particular case with which I am personally familiar is that of a Contractor developing an application for a US Government Agency that includes drawing a few graphs—just simple axes, no probability ones. This Contractor chose to use MATLAB™ as an OLE to provide the graphics, presuming that anyone using the software would have MATLAB™ installed. None of the managers or other Government employees involved with the project had MATLAB™ installed and were infuriated that the product they had paid a plenty to obtain wouldn't work. Even after a few of them purchased and installed the behemoth, they continued to have problems because none of them knew how to set up MATLAB™, another little detail the Contractor incorrectly presumed.

My advice: *Just say NO! to OLE.*

Chapter 11. Making the Most of the Clipboard

Back in Chapter 7 it was mentioned that my digitizing program will preload an image if there is one on the clipboard when it is launched. This is a good example of making the most of the clipboard. Users will save time and appreciate our applications more if they can conveniently import and export data and graphics. Create a graphic, hop over into Word®, and paste it into the document you're working on. Copy data from your Excel® spreadsheet, hop over into my curve-fitting app, fit a curve to the data, press the "create code" button, hop back over to Excel®, press Alt-F11, and paste the code implementing the curve-fit right into Excel®, and begin using it!

```
Function Y(X As Double) As Double
    Y=-1.41139306407E+001
    Y=Y*X+1.68784655694E+000
    Y=Y*X+7.33441271903E-003
End Function
```

In this chapter we will discuss how to use the clipboard with code. Before we get to the *how*, we must consider the *what*. Consider what happens when you copy a group of cells within an Excel® spreadsheet and then press Ctl-C. If you hop over to Word® and select paste special, you will see this:

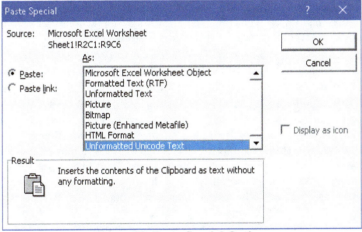

Figure 38. Paste Special Options

The first choice (Microsoft Excel Worksheet Object) might seem inappropriate for a Word document but it is not. If you were to select this option, the cells will be copied into the text in much the same way as any other table but that would not be the whole of it. If you subsequently double-click on the object, Word will launch Excel and pass this object to it. This is an example of Object Linking and Embedding (OLE) and one that actually works quite well because your version of Word and Excel are parts of the same MSO® package and will be compatible. Don't expect this same thing to work with other software.

date	day	days	words	pages
6/24/2023	Sat	1	2,350	16
6/25/2023	Sun	2	3,723	23
6/27/2023	Tue	4	4,372	25
6/28/2023	Wed	5	7,562	46
6/29/2023	Thu	6	10,306	65

Figure 39. Pasted Section of Spreadsheet

The second choice (Rich Text Format or RTF) was common decades ago before MSO became dominant in the world of Windows® but is rarely used today and very few applications recognize it. Still, there are some uses; for example, to strip off all the useless Microsoft® "decorations" in a collection of text and figures, reducing these to their generic content. Eliminating content that is recognizable only to Microsoft applications is advantageous when porting to a platform such as the WWW that is based more on UNIX than MS or others that may be more Apple-oriented. Amazon publishing, for example, will simply ignore any Microsoft-specific content.

The third choice (unformatted text) is most useful for transferring data. Note that in the case of data copied from Excel, this will be tab-delimited and any code expected to read this must handle tabs.

The fourth choice (picture) is a Device Independent Bitmap (or DIB) and works reasonably well with MSO and a few other applications but is somewhat vague and not recommended for specificity or efficiency.

The fifth choice (bitmap) is in Windows® BMP file format (less the file header, which leaves the BITMAPINFOHEADER object). This is the best choice for an image (a picture, not a line drawing, such as a graph).

The sixth choice (enhanced metafile) is a specific Windows® object. If the source was drawn (with lines and symbols as opposed to painted like a picture) the content will be a *drawing* (not a *picture*). This distinction can be very important. If you paste this drawing object into Word, you may be able to see it redraw every time the object moves, such as when scrolling, especially if it is a large object. Why this is special is that a drawing will retain fine detail when shrunken or stretched; whereas, a picture will not. The drawback with this format is that it's only recognized by MSO. No one else uses Windows Meta Files. Even Paint Shop™ converts these into drawings before displaying and manipulating them. If you need to preserve the fine detail, this is a viable option, as is HGL (Hewlett-Packard™ pen plotter format). This drawing (not a picture) data is sometimes called a *vector* format. Corel™ handles some vector formats, as does Adobe™.

The seventh choice (Hyper Text Markup Language or html) will create a table when pasted into Word® that will look just like the Excel® object but without the OLE option.

The eighth and last option (unformatted unicode text) is helpful when handling symbols outside the first 128 ASCII characters but would be very problematic were you handling data in the form of numbers.

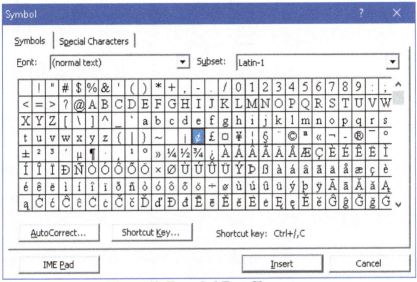

Figure 40. Extended Text Characters

Upon seeing the selection in the previous figure, you might wonder if Excel® pasted all eight types of object onto the clipboard. It didn't. The Windows® operating system starts with one or more types of objects and creates the others for you, when prompted to do so using the following command:

```
BOOL IsClipboardFormatAvailable(UINT uFormat);
```

The uFormat parameter can identify a registered clipboard format, or it can be one of the following values:

Table 11.1. Clipboard Format Options

CF_BITMAP	A handle of a bitmap (HBITMAP).
CF_DIB	A memory object containing a BITMAPINFO structure followed by the bitmap bits.
CF_DIF	Software Arts' Data Interchange Format.
CF_DSPBITMAP	Bitmap display format associated with a private format. The hData parameter must be a handle of data that can be displayed in bitmap format in lieu of the privately formatted data.

CF_DSPENHMETAFILE	Enhanced metafile display format associated with a private format. The hData parameter must be a handle of data that can be displayed in enhanced metafile format in lieu of the privately formatted data.
CF_DSPMETAFILEPICT	Metafile-picture display format associated with a private format. The hData parameter must be a handle of data that can be displayed in metafile-picture format in lieu of the privately formatted data.
CF_DSPTEXT	Text display format associated with a private format. The hData parameter must be a handle of data that can be displayed in text format in lieu of the privately formatted data.
CF_ENHMETAFILE	A handle of an enhanced metafile (HENHMETAFILE).
CF_METAFILEPICT	Handle of a metafile picture format as defined by the METAFILEPICT structure. When passing a CF_METAFILEPICT handle by means of dynamic data exchange (DDE), the application responsible for deleting hData should also free the metafile referred to by the CF_METAFILEPICT handle.
CF_OEMTEXT	Text format containing characters in the OEM character set. Each line ends with a carriage return/linefeed (CR-LF) combination. A null character signals the end of the data.
CF_OWNERDISPLAY	Owner-display format. The clipboard owner must display and update the clipboard viewer window, and receive the WM_ASKCBFORMATNAME, WM_HSCROLLCLIPBOARD, WM_PAINTCLIPBOARD, WM_SIZECLIPBOARD, and WM_VSCROLLCLIPBOARD messages. The hData parameter must be NULL.
CF_PALETTE	Handle of a color palette. Whenever an application places data in the clipboard that depends on or assumes a color palette, it should place the palette on the clipboard as well.
CF_PENDATA	Data for the pen extensions to the Microsoft® Windows™ for Pen Computing.

CF_RIFF	Represents audio data more complex than can be represented in a CF_WAVE standard wave format.
CF_SYLK	Microsoft Symbolic Link (SYLK) format.
CF_TEXT	Text format. Each line ends with a carriage return/linefeed (CR-LF) combination. A null character signals the end of the data.
CF_WAVE	Represents audio data in one of the standard wave formats, such as 11 kHz or 22 kHz pulse code modulation (PCM).
CF_TIFF	Tagged-image file format.
CF_UNICODETEXT	Unicode text format. Each line ends with a carriage return/linefeed (CR-LF) combination. A null character signals the end of the data.

If the desired format is not available, you can try sending the WM_RENDERFORMAT message:

Figure 41. WM_RENDER FORMAT

If the desired format can't be rendered by the operating system, you can try sending the WM_RENDERALLFORMATS message and then picking the best available one.

Figure 42. WM_RENDERALLFORMATS

The following code illustrates how to read numbers from text placed on the clipboard:

```
char*GetSingleDataFromClipboard()
  {
  static char*text;
  char*ht;
  int i,j,l,line;
  HGLOBAL hg;
  if(!IsClipboardFormatAvailable(CF_TEXT))
    {
    Notify("data not available","exit");
    return(NULL);
    }
  if(!OpenClipboard(NULL))
    {
```

```
      Notify("can't open clipboard","exit");
      return(NULL);
      }
   if((hg=GetClipboardData(CF_TEXT))==NULL)
      {
      Notify("can't get data","exit");
      return(NULL);
      }
   if((ht=GlobalLock(hg))==NULL)
      {
      Notify("can't lock data","exit");
      return(NULL);
      }
   l=(int)strlen(ht);
   text=calloc(l+1,sizeof(char));
   strcpy(text,ht);
   GlobalUnlock(hg);
   if(GetLastError()!=NO_ERROR)
      {
      Notify("can't unlock data","exit");
      return(NULL);
      }
   if(!CloseClipboard())
      {
      Notify("can't close clipboard","exit");
      return(NULL);
      }
   return(text);
   }
```

Note that you will need a global handle and also a pointer to an allocatable buffer to access and contain the (in this case text) data from the clipboard. Note too that you must allocate enough memory to contain the data plus a terminating zero (hence l+1 in the call to calloc). After copying the data to the local buffer, you must unlock the handle *and* close the clipboard. If any of these steps fail, you may generate a protection fault, which will crash your program. This function is designed to return NULL if the data can't be obtained from the clipboard and a pointer to a zero-terminated string if it can. Note that the resulting pointer (static char*text) must either be declared static or be outside the function at the global level; otherwise, when the function exits the pointer will be invalid because all local variables are temporarily allocated on the stack, which will be popped upon exit.

The following code snippet puts a text data buffer onto the clipboard:

```
void PutDataOnClipboard(char*data,int bytes)
   {
   char*list;
   HGLOBAL hg;
   hg=GlobalAlloc(GMEM_MOVEABLE|GMEM_DDESHARE,
```

```
    bytes);
list=GlobalLock(hg);
OpenClipboard(NULL);
EmptyClipboard()
SetClipboardData(CF_TEXT,list);
CloseClipboard();
}
```

Note that you must utilize a global handle (hg), must allocate *and* lock the buffer. You then open the clipboard, empty it, put the data on the clipboard, then close the clipboard, all separately and sequentially in this order.

While you might want to paste a common bitmap (BMP) from the clipboard into an Excel® spreadsheet or a Device Independent Bitmap (DIB), it is best to use a DIB within your own code. The reason for this is not obvious and is not prominently documented. In the context of the clipboard a BMP may or may not include a palette. If it doesn't, whoever put it on the clipboard may presume you will be using the "default" palette, which may or may not be what you think it is and may or may not correspond to what you get when you request the default palette using a call to the operating system. For this reason, you want to be clear: a DIB comes with a palette.

The following code copies a DIB (i.e., bitmap image) onto the clipboard. Note that you must allow room for the BITMAPINFOHEADER and the palette (if there is one, not for 24-bit images) and the image itself (the pixels). Note also that the Windows® rounds the length of each row up to the nearest DWORD (32-bit unsigned integer) so that w×h for 8-bit and w×h×3 for 24-bit is not necessarily the correct size.

```
BOOL PutDIB(BITMAPINFOHEADER*bh)
{
BYTE*bm;
DWORD bytes;
HGLOBAL hg;
if(bh->biBitCount==24)
  bytes=sizeof(BITMAPINFOHEADER)+bh->biSizeImage;
else
  bytes=sizeof(BITMAPINFOHEADER)+
    bh->biClrUsed*sizeof(DWORD)+bh->biSizeImage;
if((hg=GlobalAlloc(GMEM_MOVEABLE|GMEM_DDESHARE,
  bytes))==NULL)
  return(FALSE);
if((bm=GlobalLock(hg))==NULL)
  return(FALSE);
if(!OpenClipboard(NULL))
  return(FALSE);
if(!EmptyClipboard())
  return(FALSE);
if(!SetClipboardData(CF_DIB,bm))
  return(FALSE);
if(!CloseClipboard())
```

```
        return(FALSE);
    return(TRUE);
    }
```

Fetching a DIB from the clipboard within your code is quite similar but for a few modifications this code can be adapted for that purpose.

If you want to put a drawing onto the clipboard preserving each stroke and not just a picture of the drawing, which may or may not scale adequately, the best way to do this is to create an enhanced metafile in memory. To do this, you set up the process, get a handle that is compatible, draw the graph, and put it on the clipboard, as illustrated in the following code:

```
BOOL PutEMF()
    {
    HANDLE hm;
    HDC hDC;
    RECT rc;
    GetClientRect(hPlot,&rc);
    if((hDC=CreateEnhMetaFile(NULL,NULL,NULL,NULL))==NULL)
        return(FALSE);
    FillRect(hDC,&rc,WhiteBrush());
    DrawGraph(hDC,rc);
    if((hm=CloseEnhMetaFile(hDC))==NULL)
        return(FALSE);
    if(!OpenClipboard(NULL))
        return(FALSE);
    if(!EmptyClipboard())
        return(FALSE);
    if(!SetClipboardData(CF_ENHMETAFILE,hm))
        return(FALSE);
    if(!CloseClipboard())
        return(FALSE);
    return(TRUE);
    }
```

You probably want to first fill the graph with a white background using FillRect(). Draw the graph, then close the meta file. Since you probably won't have a tool that will save an enhanced meta file (i.e., vector drawing) to the disk, see the example in Appendix C.

64

Chapter 12. Working with Tabbed Windows

We have already seen three applications with tabs at the bottom in Figures 3, 13, and 30. Anyone familiar with Excel® is aware of tabs of this sort and how very useful these can be. When it comes to application development, the most common use is to provide two types of windows: text and graphics. Rather than splitting the screen space into two smaller regions, it is advantageous to place one on top of the other and switch back-and-forth between the two (or more) as needed.

While we may see this behavior in many Windows® applications, how you actually build this functionality into your own code is far from obvious and the available documentation obscure. The *tabs* window is a separate window and a child of the main window. What's inside the area framed by the tabs is the client area of the tabs window. You must also create child windows that display your content and place these inside the client rectangle of the tabs window, making each of them children of the tabs window. Furthermore, *you* must hide all of these except the one you want to appear. Windows doesn't do this for you, though it will notify you with a message when the user clicks one of the tabs. You must size all of these windows whenever anything changes to impact that. Windows or the tabs window doesn't resize the children for you. First, you must create the tabs window:

```
hTabs=CreateWindow(WC_TABCONTROL,"",
    WS_CHILD|WS_VISIBLE|WS_CLIPSIBLINGS|
    WS_CLIPCHILDREN|TCS_BOTTOM,
    0,0,0,0,hMain,NULL,hInst,NULL);
```

You must also set which font to use on the tabs. You can use one of the stock fonts or create your own, but if you do create your own, you must manage it throughout.

```
SendMessage(hTabs,WM_SETFONT,
    (WPARAM)GetStockObject(ANSI_VAR_FONT),0);
```

You must then define the tabs using a specific structure that is defined in the include file, windows.h, and set the default tab:

```
char*Tabs[]={"graphics","text",NULL};
TC_ITEM tci;
memset(&tci,0,sizeof(TC_ITEM));
tci.mask=(UINT)TCIF_TEXT;
for(i=0;Tabs[i];i++)
    {
    tci.pszText=Tabs[i];
    tci.cchTextMax=(int)strlen(Tabs[i]);
    TabCtrl_InsertItem(hTabs,i,&tci);
    }
TabCtrl_SetCurSel(hTabs,0);
```

Every time the framing changes, you must resize and reposition all of the child windows.

```
GetClientRect(hTabs,&rc);
TabCtrl_AdjustRect(hTabs,0,&rc);
MoveWindow(hPlot,0,0,rc.right,rc.bottom,TRUE);
MoveWindow(hList,0,0,rc.right,rc.bottom,TRUE);
```

Selecting a tab sends a WM_NOTIFY message to the main procedure but this isn't the only window that can generate such a message so you must check to be sure the message came from the tabs window. The handle of the window sending the message will be in the lParam, which if zero can't be the tabs window.

```
if(msg==WM_NOTIFY)
  {
  if(lParam)
    {
    HWND hFrom=((NMHDR*)lParam)->hwndFrom;
    if(hFrom==hTabs)
      {
      UINT code=((NMHDR*)lParam)->code;
      if(code==TCN_SELCHANGE)
        {
        if(TabCtrl_GetCurSel(hFrom))
          {
          ShowWindow(hPlot,SW_HIDE);
          ShowWindow(hList,SW_SHOW);
          }
        else
          {
          ShowWindow(hList,SW_HIDE);
          ShowWindow(hPlot,SW_SHOW);
          }
        }
      }
    }
  }
```

The procedure above only works when there are two tabs (either/or option). If you have more than two windows, you must either provide every possible combination or a series of loops and flags:

```
if(tab==6)
  {
  ShowWindow(hTab1,SW_HIDE);
  ShowWindow(hTab2,SW_HIDE);
  ShowWindow(hTab3,SW_HIDE);
  ShowWindow(hTab4,SW_HIDE);
  ShowWindow(hTab5,SW_HIDE);
  ShowWindow(hTab6,SW_SHOW);
  }
```

66

You may also want to switch windows some other way than with the tabs; for instance, by pushing one of the buttons to initiate some task, in which case you must hide and unhide the appropriate windows *and* change the tabs:

```
void SwitchToText(int clear)
{
TabCtrl_SetCurSel(hTabs,1);
ShowWindow(hPlot,SW_HIDE);
ShowWindow(hList,SW_SHOW);
}
void SwitchToGraphics()
{
TabCtrl_SetCurSel(hTabs,0);
ShowWindow(hList,SW_HIDE);
ShowWindow(hPlot,SW_SHOW);
}
```

Before creating a **WC_TABCONTROL** object, you must first load the common controls into memory by calling the following function (more on this later):

```
InitCommonControls();
```

Chapter 13. 3D Objects

By far the most practical way of creating, displaying, and manipulating 3D objects within a Windows® application is by using OpenGL. We only mention it in passing here because I have thoroughly covered this topic in three other books: *3D Rendering in Windows*, *3D Models in Motion*, and *3D Articulation*. One example can be seen in Figure 3. Another is shown below:

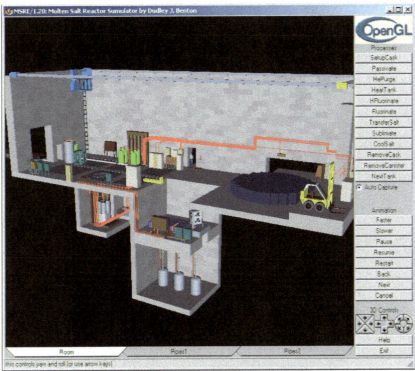

Figure 43. 3D Objects Created Using OpenGL

Chapter 14. Proprietary vs. Generic File Formats

One very annoying thing I have dealt with throughout my decades of experience with computing has been proprietary (i.e., secretive or undocumented or nontransferable) file formats. The developers of such presume you will always be using their software and that they will always be in business, neither of which is true. While the software I write can work with a variety of such formats, when I create a new format it is always generic.

Consider the plot program (TP2) shown in Figure 1. It can read 38 different types of file, which is specified by the extension (the part of the file name after the dot):

ext	contents
2DS	triangular surfaces
2DV	2D finite elements (generic)
3DS	AutoDesk™ 3D Studio™
3DV	3D finite elements (generic)
BIN	raw binary image
BMP	Windows bitmap image
CIR	colored circles
CNT	contours (raw, generic)
CON	contours (cooked, generic)
DAT	raw data
DEM	digital elevation
DSM	digital sediment
DXF	generic drawing format
F3D	3D field variable
HGL	HPGL pen plotter
MAP	painted 3D field
NDE	nodes+elements (generic)
NM8	binary animation file with details
P2D	2D polygons (generic)
P3D	3D polygons (generic)
PLT	Tecplot™ commands and/or data
PYR	3D pyramid data
RM	Raster Meta file

71

SPH colored spheres

SUR surface (cooked, generic)

TB2 2D surface (raw, generic)

TB3 3D volume (raw, generic)

TOP 2D surface (topography, generic)

TP2 TPLOT commands

TP3 3D commands + shapes

TRA triads (generic)

TRI triangles (generic)

V2D 2D vectors (generic)

V3D 3D vectors (generic)

VRM Virtual Reality Markup

WMF Windows MetaFile

WPG Word Perfect graphics

WRL Virtual Reality Markup

Think how limited an application is that will only import or export one type of file, which only work with one ridiculously expensive tool. Most projects involve multiple tools. How will you utilize data, which represents an investment of time and resources, when so very limited? 3D nodes and elements is only one type of file that in no way requires some silly proprietary format when the following will suffice:

```
600 nodes
8 3.76302 9.97396
8.17291 3.83349 9.16354
8.66174 3.89178 8.49326
9.38197 3.9278 8.079
10.2091 3.93533 7.99239
11 3.91307 8.24842
11.618 3.86486 8.80281
...
1171 elements
17 1 2
1 17 16 14
2 16 15
3 19 18
20 4 5
4 20 19
4 21 23
21 23 26
...
```

Users will also appreciate if you provide conversion from one type of file to another, as in this example:

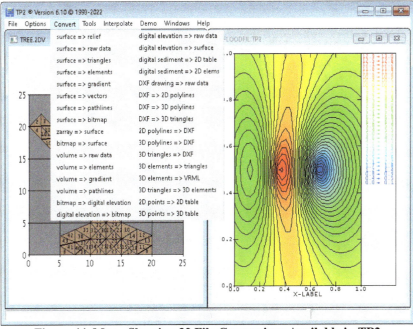

Figure 44. Menu Showing 32 File Conversions Available in TP2

These functions are not as difficult to provide as you might think:

```
char*Convert3DVtoTRI()
  {
  char*error=NULL;
  if(error=Import3DV(Dname))
    return(error);
  if(error=ExportTRI(Pname))
    {
    DestroyBody(&Body);
    return("can't create target file");
    }
  DestroyBody(&Body);
  EndConversion(TRUE);
  return(NULL);
  }
```

Chapter 15. Dialog Boxes and Data Input

Many interactive applications require some sort of data input. The classic way of accomplishing this is with what is in Windows® terminology called a *dialog* (box). We have already seen examples in this text, certainly the find-and-replace *dialog* in Word® is a familiar example. Dialogs in Visual Basic® are quite easy, which is one of the reasons the language and IDE were so popular. One might think with all the Windows® applications that dialog boxes would be routine or obvious to encode but that's not entirely the case, as we will discuss.

We first consider the most straight-forward way of creating a dialog, which is inside a resource file:

```
OPTIONS DIALOG 10,10,165,97
STYLE DS_MODALFRAME|WS_CAPTION|WS_SYSMENU|
    WS_VISIBLE|WS_POPUP
CAPTION "Options"
FONT 10,"System"
BEGIN
GROUPBOX    "Inputs",GROUP_INPUTS,3,4,95,56,WS_GROUP
EDITTEXT    EDIT_TWB,7,15,30,12,ES_AUTOHSCROLL|ES_LEFT
LTEXT       "wet-bulb [\260F]",TEXT_TWB,
    40,17,56,12,SS_LEFT
EDITTEXT    EDIT_RANGE,7,29,30,12,
    ES_AUTOHSCROLL|ES_LEFT
LTEXT       "range [\260F]",TEXT_RANGE,
    40,32,56,11,SS_LEFT
EDITTEXT    EDIT_BARO,7,44,30,12,ES_AUTOHSCROLL|ES_LEFT
LTEXT       "barometric
    [psia]",TEXT_BARO,40,46,56,12,SS_LEFT
GROUPBOX    "Method",GROUP_METHOD,103,4,57,50,WS_GROUP
CONTROL     "Merkel",RADIO_MERKEL,"Button",
    BS_AUTORADIOBUTTON|WS_GROUP,108,13,49,11
CONTROL     "Exact",RADIO_EXACT,"Button",
    BS_AUTORADIOBUTTON,108,26,49,11
CONTROL     "Crossflow",RADIO_CROSS,"Button",
    BS_AUTORADIOBUTTON,108,40,49,11
GROUPBOX    "Units",GROUP_UNITS,103,57,57,36,WS_GROUP
CONTROL     "English",RADIO_ENGLISH,"Button",
    BS_AUTORADIOBUTTON|WS_GROUP,108,66,49,11
CONTROL     "SI",RADIO_SI,"Button",BS_AUTORADIOBUTTON,
    108,79,49,11
CONTROL     "",IDC_COMBO,"Combobox",CBS_SORT|
    CBS_DROPDOWN|WS_VSCROLL|WS_TABSTOP,4,62,95,32
PUSHBUTTON  "OK",IDOK,44,80,16,12,0
END
```

The easiest way to create this application-specific script is with a tool created for this purpose (i.e., a resource editor), which comes with most any Interactive Development Environment (IDE) such as Visual Basic® or Visual Studio®. Inside the editor, this dialog box looks like:

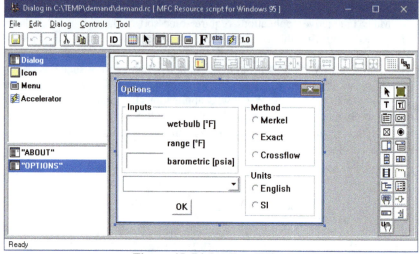

Figure 45. Dialog Box Editor

The resource file (.rc) must be compiled before the source code (.c) so that it (.res) can be linked to create the executable (.exe). In this case the commands are:

```
rc /v demand.rc
cl /Ox /W3 /WX demand.c moistair.c demand.res
    user32.lib gdi32.lib comdlg32.lib
```

An important distinction between dialog box function in the context of the Windows® operating system is *modeness*. A *modal* dialog box must be closed before the application can continue (i.e., *control* is taken away from the main message handling loop and given over to the dialog message handling loop). A *modeless* dialog box can receive input and dispatch messages while the main program is doing something else. These terms (modal and modeless) are not used this way in any other context, as a Google™ search will reveal.

This is a *modal* dialog box. When it comes time to launch it (we select *options* from the main menu), we call the following:

```
if(wParam==PUSH_OPTIONS)
    {
    ModalDialog("OPTIONS",(DLGPROC)OptionsProc,0,hMain);
    SetFocus(hMain);
    RedrawWindow(hPlot,NULL,NULL,
        RDW_INVALIDATE|RDW_ERASE);
    return(FALSE);
    }
```

We supply the name from the resource file ("OPTIONS") and a user-defined function (OptionsProc), along with the handle of the program yielding control (hMain). The main program stops here and does not resume to the

SetFocus() call until after the *modal* dialog box is closed. We must set the keyboard focus back to the main program, otherwise keystrokes will be sent to oblivion, as the dialog window. Also, we must redraw (or repaint) the window beneath the dialog when it disappears and uncovers it. The user-defined procedure looks like this:

```
LRESULT WINAPI OptionsProc(HWND hWnd,DWORD msg,
   WPARAM wParam,LPARAM lParam)
{
if(msg==WM_CLOSE)
   return(EndDialog(hWnd,IDCANCEL));
if(msg==WM_COMMAND)
   {
   if((HWND)lParam==GetDlgItem(hWnd,IDC_COMBO))
      {
      if(HIWORD(wParam)==CBN_SELENDOK)
         if(GetOpenFile(data.name,"*.*\000*.*\000",
            "fill data file"))
            ReadData();
      return(FALSE);
      }
   if(HIWORD(wParam)==BN_CLICKED||
      HIWORD(wParam)==BN_DOUBLECLICKED)
      {
      if(LOWORD(wParam)==IDOK||LOWORD(wParam)==IDCANCEL)
         {
         GetOptions(hWnd);
         return(EndDialog(hWnd,LOWORD(wParam)));
         }
      if(LOWORD(wParam)==RADIO_CROSS   ||
         LOWORD(wParam)==RADIO_ENGLISH||
         LOWORD(wParam)==RADIO_EXACT   ||
         LOWORD(wParam)==RADIO_MERKEL ||
         LOWORD(wParam)==RADIO_SI)
         {
         GetOptions(hWnd);
         SetOptions(hWnd);
         }
      }
   else if(HIWORD(wParam)==EN_KILLFOCUS)
      {
      double val;
      val=GetDlgItemTextValue(hWnd,LOWORD(wParam));
      SetDlgItemTxt(hWnd,LOWORD(wParam),"%lG",val);
      }
   return(FALSE);
   }
if(msg==WM_CTLCOLORBTN)
   {
   SetBkMode((HDC)wParam,TRANSPARENT);
```

77

```
SetTextColor((HDC)wParam,BLACK);
return((LRESULT)GetStockObject(LTGRAY_BRUSH));
}
if(msg==WM_CTLCOLORDLG)
  return((LRESULT)GetStockObject(LTGRAY_BRUSH));
if(msg==WM_CTLCOLOREDIT)
{
SetTextColor((HDC)wParam,0x000000);
return((LRESULT)GetStockObject(WHITE_BRUSH));
}
if(msg==WM_CTLCOLORSTATIC)
{
SetBkMode((HDC)wParam,TRANSPARENT);
SetTextColor((HDC)wParam,BLACK);
return((LRESULT)GetStockObject(LTGRAY_BRUSH));
}
if(msg==WM_INITDIALOG)
{
char*text[]={"no data file selected",
  "select data file",NULL};
int i;
CenterWindowOnScreen(hWnd);
BringWindowToTop(hWnd);
SetOptions(hWnd);
for(i=0;text[i];i++)
  SendDlgItemMessage(hWnd,IDC_COMBO,
    CB_ADDSTRING,0,(LPARAM)text[i]);
SendDlgItemMessage(hWnd,IDC_COMBO,CB_SETCURSEL,0,0);
return(TRUE);
}
return(FALSE);
}
```

If this seems complicated, it is, because you must specifically handle every message that is sent to the dialog, including: create, destroy, paint (each element, including text), what shape cursor to use where (+, →, _, etc.). You must even bring the dialog to the top and center it on the screen, because Windows doesn't do this for you. Note this section:

```
if(HIWORD(wParam)==CBN_SELENDOK)
  if(GetOpenFile(data.name,"*.*\000*.*\000",
    "fill data file"))
    ReadData();
return(FALSE);
```

Here we open a file and read it. As this is not a message-driven process and does not specifically depend on Windows® to do anything, it will proceed, regardless of the fact that we are currently stuck inside the dialog message loop at this time and the main message loop has been suspended.

The final result looks like this:

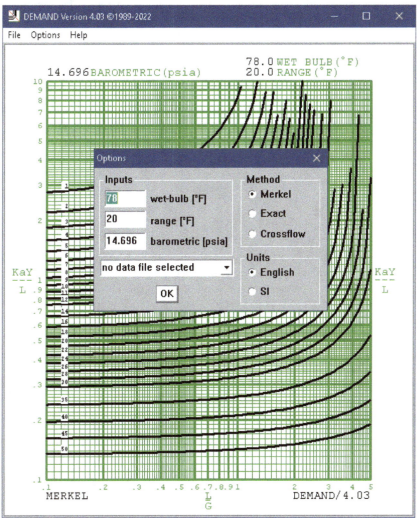

Figure 46. Modal Dialog Atop Main Application Window

<u>Enter vs. Tab Advance</u>

There is an additional feature here not covered in any Windows® documentation I have ever seen. Every other Windows application that accepts line-by-line data entry (think Excel®), when you type in a number and press the Enter key, advances to the next box—but this doesn't! If you type in a number and press the Tab key, Windows will advance the cursor (and keyboard focus) to the next box so why not when you press Enter? Who presses Tab to drop *down* to the next box? When we press Tab in Excel, it advances to the right, not down. Why this functionality isn't built into Windows, nobody knows. Thankfully, you can build it in and your users will thank you for it. In fact, little details like this will keep them coming back to you for more work.

As it turns out, pressing the Enter key sends a notification to the *main* message loop, which is supposed to be suspended. This is why the *dialog* message loop never sees it. How do we fix this annoying oversight? By intercepting the letter, changing the name on the envelope, change the Enter to a Tab, and mailing to the person who should have received it:

```
while(GetMessage(&msg,NULL,0,0))
  {
  if(msg.hwnd==hDialog)
    if(msg.message==WM_KEYDOWN)
      if(msg.wParam==VK_ENTER)
        PostMessage(hDialog,WM_COMMAND,VK_TAB,0);
    if(!TranslateMessage(&msg))
      DispatchMessage(&msg);
  }
```

One tiny detail that might be overlooked is that we must save the handle to the dialog box (hDialog) in global memory (in the program but outside the individual functions); otherwise, we wouldn't know this inside the main message loop to check for it.

Chapter 16. Text Output and List Boxes

Applications often involve text, not just data in the form of text, but additional information, including: intermediate values, iterative progress, summary results, and more. While this information could be written to a simple (in Windows® terminology WS_STATIC) window, the best way to present this information is in what Windows® calls a LISTBOX.

While tabs are an integral part of the Windows® operating system and a foundational element of the user interface, these aren't available by default. Tabs are one of several objects called *common controls*. This group consists of two subgroups of controls referred to as *stock* and *extended*. The stock subgroup includes: BUTTON, COMBOBOX, EDIT, LISTBOX, MDICLIENT, SCROLLBAR, and STATIC. The extended subgroup includes: ANIMATE, DRAGLIST, HEADER, HOTKEY, IMAGELIST, LISTVIEW, MENUHELP, PROGRESS, STATUSBAR, TABCONTROL, TOOLBAR, TRACKBAR, TREEVIEW, and UPDOWN. In order to use one of these controls in your program, you simply create a window using the *name* as the *class*, for example:

```
hList=CreateWindow("LISTBOX",NULL,
   WS_CHILD|WS_VISIBLE|WS_BORDER|WS_VSCROLL|
   LBS_DISABLENOSCROLL|LBS_HASSTRINGS|
   LBS_NOINTEGRALHEIGHT|LBS_USETABSTOPS,
   0,0,0,0,hTabs,0,hInst,NULL);
```

You must include all of the *styles* (appearance factors) you want this control to have (it is a child of the main window, it will be visible, it will have a border, etc.). You must also size the window at some point, which will require knowledge of the space available in the client area of the main window. This will not be known until after the main window is created because different versions of the operating system and differing options for the appearance impact the size of borders and titles and other details, which can be obtained by calling another library function:

```
icon.w=GetSystemMetrics(SM_CXICON)
icon.h=GetSystemMetrics(SM_CYICON)
```

Even though these controls are part of the Windows® interface and operating system, you must first call a function to load the class definitions and associated procedures before creating a window of this type:

```
InitCommonControls();
```

If you don't call this before creating the windows (i.e., control objects), the CreateWindow() function will fail.

You will need to specify a vertical scrollbar and that the control will receive strings with the options: WS_VSCROLL and LBS_HASSTRINGS. Note that the vertical scroll is a Windows (WS_) style and the strings are a listbox (LBS_) style. If you want the vertical scroll bar and button to appear all the time (whether or not the text extends beyond the viewing area), you can add the LBS_DISABLENOSCROLL style. (It's a double negative: don't disable the

81

scrollbar.) If you want the text to appear smoothly, even when part of a line is obscured, you can add the **LBS_NOINTEGRALHEIGHT** style. (Word®, for example, will display part of an obscured line and this is the more common expectation for appearance.) If you want to use tabs to align text, you can also include the **LBS_USETABSTOPS** option, but you must then define the tabs and use them appropriately. (Also note that tabs in a Windows control don't work and are pointless with variable-pitch fonts, so you will need to select a font that does work:

```
hF=GetStockObject(ANSI_FIXED_FONT);
hF=GetStockObject(ANSI_VAR_FONT)
```

Writing information into a LISTBOX is not exactly like writing it to a text file or the console using printf(...). For one thing, a LISTBOX doesn't recognize the linefeed (LF or \n) or carriage return (CR or \r). You put text into a LISTBOX by sending a message:

```
SendMessage(hList,LB_ADDSTRING,0,(LONG)text);
```

which will occupy a single line, whether there is a \n or \r at the end of the text or not. When using printf() you can *build* a line of text using several calls to printf() before sending a \n or \r, but this is not the case with a LISTBOX. Also, you cannot send a message with a format like:

```
printf("x=%lG\n",x);
```

You can, however create a function that will work just like printf() so that you can adapt existing code to your LISTBOX or simply program in the same way that you would if you were writing to a file or the console:

```
void printl(char*format,...)
  {
  char bufr[1024];
  va_list arg_marker;
  va_start(arg_marker,format);
  if(vsprintf(bufr,format,arg_marker)>=sizeof(bufr))
    FatalAppExit(0,"AddText(): buffer overflow");
  SendMessage(hList,LB_ADDSTRING,0,(LONG)bufr);
  }
```

This is an example of what the end result looks like:

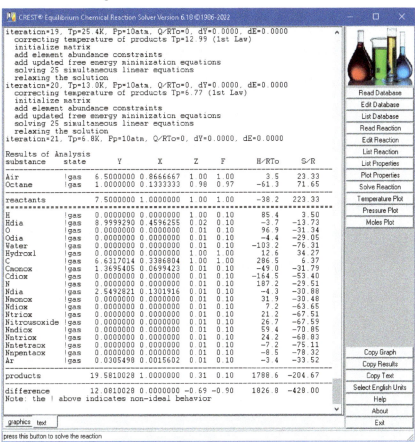

Figure 47. Example LISTBOX Output

Chapter 17. Managing Mouse Messages

Drawing text and lines in a window are easy enough (see Appendix D) but managing mouse messages to work with this information is significantly more complicated. When clicking about in a child window of type WS_STATIC, mouse messages will be sent to the main message loop, that is: MainProc() or whatever you named it. This is because the procedure associated with class "STATIC" windows is part of the operating system and has built in the logic to receive such messages and forward them to the main window message loop.

If, however, you are clicking about in a child window of a user-defined class, say "PLOT", associated with a procedure, say PlotProc(), then the messages will be sent to the user-defined procedure and you must handle them. The following code is one example:

```
int WINAPI PlotProc(HWND hWnd,DWORD msg,WPARAM
    wParam,LPARAM lParam)
{
if(msg==WM_CLOSE)
   return(FALSE);
if(msg==WM_CREATE)
   return(FALSE);
if(msg==WM_DESTROY)
   return(FALSE);
```

You must process (or at least respond correctly) to these three basic messages.

```
if(msg==WM_LBUTTONDOWN)
   {
   if(IsWindowVisible(hWnd))
      return(LeftButtonDown(wParam,lParam));
   else
      return(FALSE);
   }
if(msg==WM_LBUTTONUP)
   {
   if(IsWindowVisible(hWnd))
      return(LeftButtonUp(wParam,lParam));
   else
      return(FALSE);
   }
```

You can provide your own separate functions (in this case LeftButtonDown and LeftButtonUp) to organize and simplify the flow of coding.

```
if(msg==WM_MOUSEMOVE)
   {
   if(IsWindowVisible(hWnd))
      {
      if(wParam&MK_LBUTTON)
         return(LeftButtonMove(wParam,lParam));
      else if(wParam&MK_RBUTTON)
```

85

```
    return(RightButtonMove(wParam,lParam));
  else
    return(FALSE);
  }
else
  return(FALSE);
}
```

You will receive a message whenever the mouse is moved over this window.

```
if(msg==WM_PAINT)
  {
  HDC hDC;
  PAINTSTRUCT pS;
  if(IsWindowVisible(hWnd))
    {
    hDC=BeginPaint(hWnd,&pS);
    DrawPolygons();
    EndPaint(hWnd,&pS);
    return(FALSE);
    }
  else
    return(FALSE);
  }
```

You must repaint the entire window when necessary.

```
if(msg==WM_RBUTTONDOWN)
  {
  if(IsWindowVisible(hWnd))
    return(RightButtonDown(wParam,lParam));
  else
    return(FALSE);
  }
if(msg==WM_RBUTTONUP)
  {
  if(IsWindowVisible(hWnd))
    return(RightButtonUp(wParam,lParam));
  else
    return(FALSE);
  }
if(msg==WM_SIZE)
  {
  PositionWindows(0,0);
  return(FALSE);
  }
```

You will get a separate message for each combination of mouse input. Don't forget to pass any message you didn't handle to the default procedure.

```
    return(DefWindowProc(hWnd,msg,wParam,lParam));
  }
```

Dragging the mouse is more complicated. You might think that were you to drag a rectangle over part of the window (as shown below) that Windows® would send you a handy little message with the coordinates of the enclosed rectangle... but you'd be wrong. You must keep track of where the mouse was, which button was pushed, where it was dragged to, whether the same button was still pushed, and whether or not the button was released—all separate and different messages. If the user begins but doesn't complete the process, you must keep track of that too. Furthermore, you don't want to keep these in a growing stack of such message information because you must perform the indicated tasks as they are communicated by the user through the mouse.

Figure 48. Example of Mouse Drag Rectangle

Another little detail we should mention here is the ambiguity over where the point (0,0) is within an image or on the screen within a window. You will quickly discover your mistake if you paint an image or draw a graph and it's upside down. In the real world (outside computers and Windows® in particular), (0,0) is always the bottom left corner (like the Equator and Greenwich Mean Time or any other map or graph that has ever been drawn). Inside Windows® the point (0,0) is the upper left corner. This goes for MoveTo(), LineTo(), and mouse messages, so when you're creating a graph, you must constantly shift back-and-forth between user-perspective coordinates and Window coordinates.

All the bookkeeping necessary to handle and combine multiple mouse messages (including left click down, drag, left click up) is why it may be less confusing to create individual functions for each and call these from the message loop in the PlotProc() as they are received, for example (sorry it's so long but it's all very necessary):

```
struct{int down,move,pend,save,x1,x2,y1,y2;}mouse;
int WINAPI LeftButtonDown(WPARAM wParam,LPARAM lParam)
  {
  mouse.x1=mouse.x2=LOSHORT(lParam);
  mouse.y1=mouse.y2=HISHORT(lParam);
  mouse.down=wParam;
  mouse.move=mouse.pend=mouse.save=0;
  SetCapture(hPlot);
  if(Selected.n>0)
     {
     if(mouse.down&MK_CONTROL)
        mouse.pend=-1;
     else
        SelectPolygons(mouse.x1,mouse.y1,
           mouse.x2,mouse.y2);
     }
  }
  return(FALSE);
  }
int WINAPI LeftButtonMove(WPARAM wParam,LPARAM lParam)
  {
  RECT rc;
  if(!(mouse.down&MK_LBUTTON))
     return(FALSE);
  if(mouse.pend>0)
     {
     if(mouse.pend>1)
        {
        DrawPolygons();
        mouse.pend=1;
        }
     mouse.x1=mouse.x2;
     mouse.y1=mouse.y2;
     mouse.x2=LOSHORT(lParam);
     mouse.y2=HISHORT(lParam);
```

You must get and save the mouse data. The position (x,y) is packed into a single DWORD (unsigned 32-bit value) but as two *signed* integers.

```
     DrawPolygon(Selected.p);
     }
  else if(mouse.pend<0)
     {
```

```
mouse.x1=mouse.x2;
mouse.y1=mouse.y2;
mouse.x2=LOSHORT(lParam);
mouse.y2=HISHORT(lParam);
   mouse.save=1;
InvalidateRect(hPlot,NULL,TRUE);
```
You must tell Windows to repaint inside the polygon after altering it with your mouse drag box, which *you* had to specifically draw. Windows doesn't do this for you!
```
}
else if(!(mouse.down&MK_CONTROL))
{
if(mouse.move)
   {
   rc.left  =min(mouse.x1,mouse.x2);
   rc.right =max(mouse.x1,mouse.x2);
   rc.top   =min(mouse.y1,mouse.y2);
   rc.bottom=max(mouse.y1,mouse.y2);
   InvertFrame(pDC,&rc);
   }
mouse.x2=LOSHORT(lParam);
mouse.y2=HISHORT(lParam);
mouse.move++;
rc.left  =min(mouse.x1,mouse.x2);
rc.right =max(mouse.x1,mouse.x2);
rc.top   =min(mouse.y1,mouse.y2);
rc.bottom=max(mouse.y1,mouse.y2);
InvertFrame(pDC,&rc);
}
return(FALSE);
}
```
You must handle the down click *and* the up click!
```
int WINAPI LeftButtonUp(WPARAM wParam,LPARAM lParam)
{
int p;
RECT rc;
if(!(mouse.down&MK_LBUTTON))
   return(FALSE);
if(mouse.down&MK_CONTROL)
   return(FALSE);
mouse.x2=LOSHORT(lParam);
mouse.y2=HISHORT(lParam);
if(mouse.move)
   {
   rc.left  =min(mouse.x1,mouse.x2);
   rc.right =max(mouse.x1,mouse.x2);
   rc.top   =min(mouse.y1,mouse.y2);
   rc.bottom=max(mouse.y1,mouse.y2);
```

```
InvertFrame(pDC,&rc);
if(mouse.down&MK_SHIFT)
  {
  for(p=0;p<Np;p++)
    if(Poly[p].select<0)
      Poly[p].select=1;
  SelectRectangle(mouse.x1,mouse.y1,
    mouse.x2,mouse.y2);
  InvalidateRect(hPlot,NULL,TRUE);
```

You must invalidate the rectangle (inform Windows that it must be redrawn).

```
  }
else
  {
  DeSelectAll();
  SelectRectangle(mouse.x1,mouse.y1,
    mouse.x2,mouse.y2);
  InvalidateRect(hPlot,NULL,TRUE);
  }
}
else if(mouse.pend>0)
  InvalidateRect(hPlot,NULL,TRUE);
mouse.down=0;
mouse.move=0;
ReleaseCapture();
UpdateButtons();
return(FALSE);
}
```

Furthermore, *you* must control the keyboard focus using the SetCapture(), GetCapture(), and ReleaseCapture(); otherwise, the user will be tapping and clicking and cursing the programmer when the whole thing seemingly locks up because the keyboard focus has gone off to la la land.

After you process all the mouse messages and figure out which polygons the user has selected, you must redraw everything to show the selection. Windows does *not* do this for you! Windows doesn't draw a line or point differently just because you set a flag indicating the selection. You must use a different color, maybe a different width line, and perhaps a little box to show the individual points.

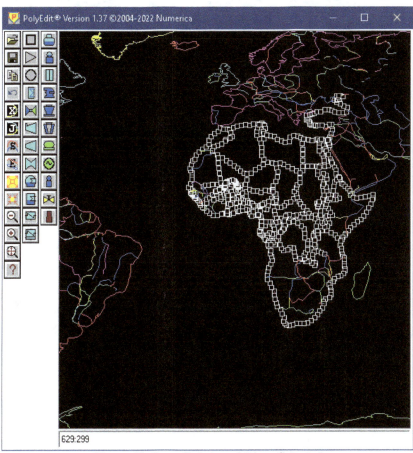

Figure 49. Some Points and Lines Selected

Let's say you want to select a single point and drag it somewhere else. You must process every one of those possible mouse messages and that's why the sample code above is so long and complicated and why we create a special data structure to handle all that information. After detecting the user's mouse clicks indicating a single point has been chosen, you must sift through every point to see if it lies in the area beneath the click (+). Then you must keep track of where the user drags it to, gathering information along the way, and swapping back-

91

and-forth between screen coordinates and map coordinates, which are not likely to ever be the same.

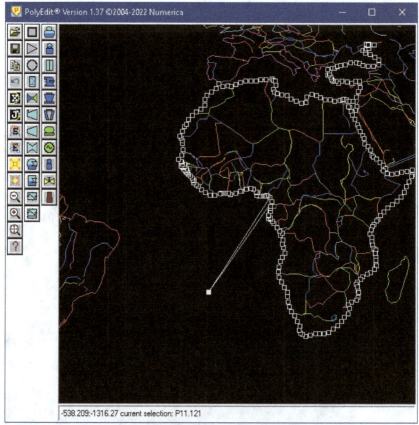

Figure 50. Click-and-Drag a Point

You may also want to drag Madagascar out into the South Atlantic Ocean or more likely a pump or other component in a drawing to somewhere else. That's why you must keep track of whether the control key was down when the user dragged the mouse or selected the points:

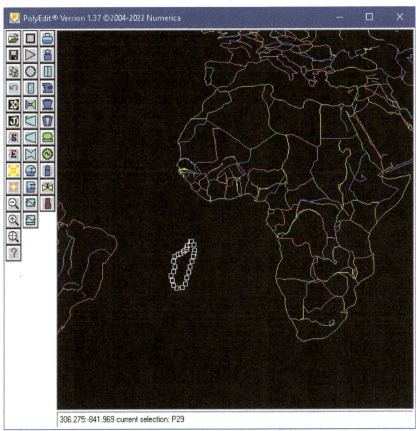

Figure 51. Click-and-Drag a Polygon

<u>Short-Cut Keys Will Be Very Much Appreciated</u>

Users will flock to your door if you can turn a complicated hassle into a single keystroke. You define the hot keys in an accelerator table as before in Chapter 8. Then you write a little function to perform each task and call the appropriate one when the WM_COMMAND message is sent to the main message loop with the ID of the hotkey. Here is a list of such short cuts that the polygon editor shown in these figures can handle.

PolyEdit Shortcut Keys

    Alt-A inverts the current selection
    Alt-B make the selected point the first in selected polygon

Alt-C closes all open selected polygons
Alt-D deletes the current selection
Alt-E changes the point spacing for all selected polygons
Alt-F selects the first point in the selected polygon
Alt-G "grow" or increase in size
Alt-H sort points horizontally (along X) in a single polygon
Alt-J joins two open selected polygons
Alt-K "shrink" or decrease in size
Alt-L selects the last point in the selected polygon
Alt-N selects the next point in the selected polygon
Alt-O opens all closed selected polygons
Alt-P selects the previous point in the selected polygon
Alt-Q squares the corner of the selected polygon at the selected point
Alt-R renames a single selected object
Alt-S smooths all selected polygons
Alt-T deletes selected polygons shorter than specified length
Alt-V reverses selected polygon
Alt-X splits selected polygon at selected point
Alt-Y sort points along Y (vertically) in a single polygon
Alt-Z optimizes all selected polygons
Alt-backspace undo the last change
Ctrl-A select all polygons
Ctrl-C copys current selection to clipboard
Ctrl-F flip (top/bottom)
Ctrl-J joins all overlapping selected polygons
Ctrl-M mirror (left/right)
Ctrl-N creates a new polygon
Ctrl-O opens a new file
Ctrl-Q squares the corner of the selected polygon at the selected point
Ctrl-R rotate (clockwise 90°)
Ctrl-S save and continue
Ctrl-V pastes from clipboard
Ctrl-X cuts current selection to clipboard
Ctrl-Z resets the zoom and pan to full view
Ctrl-Alt-F first polygon
Ctrl-Alt-L last polygon
Ctrl-Alt-N next polygon
Ctrl-Alt-P previous polygon
Select a single point on a single polygon, then push: Alt-Left, Alt-Right, Alt-Up, or Alt-Down to move that point a single pixel in the indicated direction.

Forty commands in all, accomplishing each task with a single keystroke. While you can edit polygons (drawings, maps, contours) in AutoCAD™, it will be slower than a herd of snails stampeding up the side of a salt dome compared to PolyEdit. That's why I created this delightful program. On many projects we had to work with polygons. Elevation contours on a job site were often provided as AutoCAD™ drawings but we needed the information digitized—not just as a pretty picture but as x,y,z polygons for building 3D surfaces such as this:

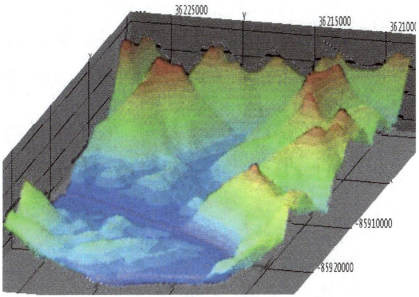

Figure 52. Topography from Elevation Contour Polygons

Or vectors showing the direction of surface runoff:

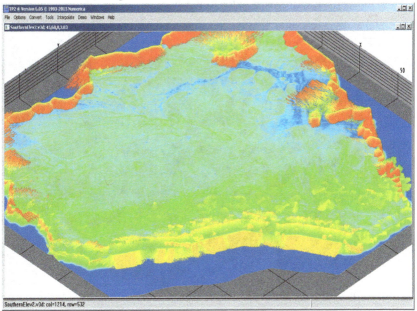

Figure 53. Surface Run-Off Vectors

With just a few keystrokes, we can flip, mirror, and expand Australia to fill up the Pacific Ocean:

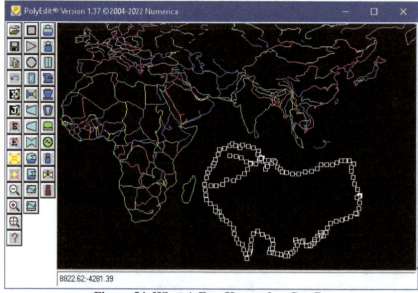

Figure 54. What A Few Keystrokes Can Do

While we might not want to move Australia, we will want to use these shortcuts to modify objects in other types of drawings.

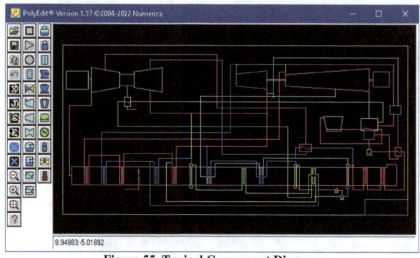

Figure 55. Typical Component Diagram

Chapter 18. Making the Most of the Status Bar

Many windows have a status bar at the bottom that notifies the user of various information from the position in a file to the current time. A STATUSBAR is one of the extended common controls listed in Chapter 16. Add a status bar to your application by calling:

```
RECT rc;
InitCommonControls();
GetClientRect(hMain,&rc);
hStat=CreateWindow(STATUSCLASSNAME,NULL,
    WS_CHILD|WS_VISIBLE|WS_CLIPSIBLINGS,
    0,rc.bottom-20,rc.right,20,hMain,0,hInst,NULL);
```

You must position the status bar within the client area of main window, usually at the bottom, which means you must get the client rectangle to calculate the position. A typical height is 20 pixels, which leaves room for the border and text. You can just use the default font or specify a font by sending a message to the window:

```
SendMessage(hStat,WM_SETFONT,
    (WPARAM)GetStockObject(ANSI_VAR_FONT),0);
```

Update the contents of the status bar (presuming it is text) by calling:

```
SetWindowText(hStat,text);
```

It can be very helpful to show in the status bar what a button will do if you push it. You can use mouse messages sent to the main procedure to key these notifications for the user:

```
while(GetMessage(&msg,NULL,0,0))
  {
  if(msg.message==WM_MOUSEMOVE||msg.message
    ==WM_NCMOUSEMOVE)
  {
  if(msg.hwnd==hTabs)
    SetWindowText(hStat,"change the view");
  else if(msg.hwnd==hEdit)
    SetWindowText(hStat,"edit the database");
  else if(msg.hwnd==hListDb)
    SetWindowText(hStat,"list the database");
  else if(msg.hwnd==hSolve)
    SetWindowText(hStat,"solve reaction");
  else
```

Chapter 19. Oops! How Do I Undo That?

Windows® does not provide any functionality for *undo* in your applications. While this is a common feature in many applications that run on the Windows operating system, this behavior is left entirely up to the programmer. Obviously, some applications need this more than others. My polygon editor, for example, would be a nightmare without *undo*. While there may be many ways of implementing *undo*, I have found it most efficient to 1) keep it all in memory (as opposed to writing it out to a file) and 2) keep it all on a *stack*.

A *stack* (in the programming sense) refers to a growing list of items. Perhaps the aspect that makes the discussion of stacks unique is the order, which we call: last-in, first-out. The term *stack* comes from the physical reference to cafeteria trays:

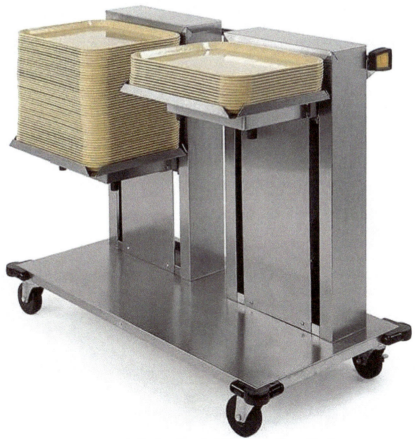

Figure 56. Spring-Loaded Cafeteria Tray Stack

99

You *push* objects onto the stack (at the top) and *pop* them off the stack (also from the top and never the bottom). If you want to *undo* some actions, before you make a change, you push the *opposite* onto the stack. When the user issues an *undo* command (by pushing a button or pressing Alt-backspace if you have added this to the accelerator table), you *pop* the last thing off the stack and *do* it. If, for instance, the user presses Alt-G in PolyEdit, the selected polygon(s) *grow* (i.e., get bigger by a factor of 1.1). We first push a *shrink* (get smaller by a factor of 1.1) command onto the stack and then *grow* the polygon(s). The undo in this case pops a shrink command off the stack, which effectively reverses the previous change.

We must also keep track of which polygons were selected at the time the first command was issued. The undo process must deselect the current polygon(s) if any, select the previous one(s), shrink them, deselect them, reselect what was the current group, and redraw everything. This means that we must have what are effectively *internal* messages (e.g., shrink, grow, select, etc.) that indicate what we did or need to do. This should include a "do nothing" message and also "nothing left to do" message. We can easily define these using enum because the values don't matter.

```
enum{begin=-1,delete_point,insert_point,replace_point,
    begin_polygon,close_polygon,close_polygons,
    delete_polygon,delete_polygons,flip_polygon,
    flip_polygons,grow_polygon,grow_polygons,
    insert_polygon,insert_polygons,mirror_polygon,
    mirror_polygons,open_polygon,open_polygons,
    rename_polygon,replace_polygon,replace_polygons,
    reverse_polygon,reverse_polygons,rotate_polygon,
    rotate_polygons,shrink_polygon,shrink_polygons,
    unmodified,zoom};
```

As we must save some bytes, integers, double-precision floating-point real numbers, and perhaps other objects, I have found it most efficient to have one code that pushes bytes and another that pops bytes. The byte pushing function must reallocate memory as needed but this is not required when popping. Each of the other objects can be assembled from one or more bytes, eliminating the necessity for lengthy code to handle each type. For example:

```
void PushByte(BYTE b)
{
if(undo.n>=undo.m)
  {
  undo.m+=1024;

  undo.b=reallocate(undo.b,undo.n,undo.m,sizeof(BYTE));
  }
if(undo.n==0)
  {
  ButtonEnable(bUndo,TRUE);
  UpdateButtons();
```

100

```
    }
undo.b[undo.n++]=b;
}
```

If there is nothing to undo, then disable the undo button if there is one. There is no reallocate() function in current versions of Windows, although there was one many, many years ago. You must provide this too:

```
void*reallocate(void*old_ptr,unsigned long old_count,
    unsigned long new_count,unsigned size)
{
void*new_ptr;
if((new_ptr=malloc(max(1024,new_count*size)))==NULL)
    FatalAppExit(0,"can't allocate memory");
memset(new_ptr,0,new_count*size);
if(old_ptr!=NULL)
    {
    memcpy(new_ptr,old_ptr,min(old_count,
        new_count)*size);
    free(old_ptr);
    }
return(new_ptr);
}
```

Note that some versions of Windows will not properly allocate less than 1k of memory so that we use the max(1024,...) to avoid this problem. When reallocating (i.e., expanding) memory, you must first allocate more, copy the existing data into the new space, release the old space, and return a pointer to the new. We recover data (bytes) from the stack with this code:

```
BYTE PopByte()
{
if(undo.n<1)
    FatalAppExit(0,"stack underflow");
return(undo.b[--undo.n]);
}
```

We push and pop a 32-bit integer with the following code:

```
void PushInt(int i)
{
union{BYTE b[2];int i;}u;
u.i=i;
PushByte(u.b[0]);
PushByte(u.b[1]);
}
int PopInt()
{
union{BYTE b[2];int i;}u;
u.b[1]=PopByte();
u.b[0]=PopByte();
return(u.i);
}
```

101

Note the reverse order between pushing and popping. We do the same thing for double-precision floating-point values, which are 32-bits or 8 bytes:

```
void PushDouble(double d)
  {
  int i;
  union{BYTE b[8];double d;}u;
  u.d=d;
  for(i=0;i<8;i++)
    PushByte(u.b[i]);
  }
double PopDouble()
  {
  int i;
  union{BYTE b[8];double d;}u;
  for(i=7;i>=0;i--)
    u.b[i]=PopByte();
  return(u.d);
  }
```

In order to save a polygon or other complex object we combine several calls, including some sort of flag:

```
void PushPolygon(double*x,double*y,int n)
  {
  int i;
  for(i=n-1;i>=0;i--)
    {
    PushDouble(y[i]);
    PushDouble(x[i]);
    }
  PushInt(n);
  PushByte(its_a_polygon);
```

Note that we push the coordinates on first in reverse order, then the count, then the flag so that when we want to recover the polygon, we first get the flag that tells us what it is:

```
typedef struct{int n;double*x,*y;}POLY;
POLY PopPolygon()
  {
  int i;
  static POLY p;
  p.n=PopInt();
  p.x=calloc(2*n,sizeof(double));
  p.y=p.x+n;
  for(i=n-1;i>=0;i--)
    {
    p.x[i]=PopDouble();
    p.y[i]=PopDouble();
    }
  return(p);
  }
```

Note that we *must* declare the POLY structure inside this function type *static* because Windows (or Intel processors responding the way machine language is created from the code) does not preserve the information on the *processor stack*. (This has nothing to do with our stack). When control returns from a function (this is inside the processor) to the calling point, if a BYTE is returned, it will be stored in the AL register, and so forth for a WORD in the AX register, a DWORD in either the AX:DX registers or the EAX register (depending on the current operating mode), or a QWORD in the EAX:EDX or RAX register (depending on the current operating mode). These are all hardware registers inside the processor and not in memory somewhere so that they don't *disappear* when the *processor stack* is popped returning from a function call. Larger items must be returned in memory somewhere (depending on the compiler design and settings) and this had better not be in the function we just left because that's gone as far as the processor is concerned. Floating-point return values are left at the top of the FPU stack so we don't need to worry about returning a single floating-point number (whether single- or double-precision).

The only time this problem (returning something larger than the size of a register) is when we return a static string, such as:

```
char*DoSomething()
  {
  if(there_is_a_problem)
    return("can't do it!");
  do it
  return(NULL);
  }
  if((err=DoSomething())!=NULL)
    FatalAppExit(0,err);
```

This isn't a problem because the string "can't do it!" is either in the code segment or the global data segment depending on the compiler design and settings; so, while it may seem *local* to the function, it isn't.

Appendix A. C Compilers

Everything you need to build applications written in C for the Windows® operating system can be obtained without cost. There are several compilers that you can find on the Internet. They each have different strengths and weaknesses.

The Microsoft® C Compiler

Download and install the Windows® Software Development Kit (SDK) and Driver Development Kit (DDK). Combine the folders and begin compiling. Visual Studio® is an Interactive Development and Debugging Environment (IDDE) and is entirely superfluous. The C compiler, resource compiler, and linker all come with the SDK and DDK. This compiler comes in 4 configurations based on two options (32-bit or 64-bit). The four options are: 1) run on a 32-bit machine and create 32-bit executables, 2) run on a 32-bit machine but create 64-bit executables, 3) run on a 64-bit machine but create 32-bit executables, and 4) run on a 64-bit machine and create 64-bit executables. You will need at least two of these if you intend to create XLLs for Excel®; otherwise, the 32/32 will work. The situations where a 64-bit executable is *necessary* are exceedingly rare, mostly if you need more than 2GB of memory in a single program.

The Digital Mars C Compiler

Walter Bright wrote the first ever single-pass C^{++} compiler. It was called Zortech®. Symantec® picked it up for several years but dumped it when they realized it wasn't profitable. Walter Bright retained the rights and you can now download this excellent compiler for free off the Internet. The Digital Mars C compiler will only create 32-bit native executables. There are no plans at this time to add 64-bit capability.

Walter Bright's compilers don't optimize code as tightly as the Microsoft® compiler, but it is much more reliable. For the first two decades of its existence, the Microsoft® *optimizing* C compiler was very slow and buggy. There have been considerable improvements so that it is now faster and more reliable.

The most amazing feature of Walter Bright's compilers is the *generate trace* functionality that is activated with the -gt option. When this option is activated the application runs very slowly, but when it's done, it leaves behind a list (TRACE.LOG) of every function, how many times it was called, by what other function, and how long it took. You can use this information to optimize and structure your code.

Other C Compilers

While some of the Gnu® tools and code can be made to function on the Windows® platform, you will find this quite a hassle. Everything Gnu® is developed within an entirely different framework and mindset. It can be done, but you will waste a lot of time doing it. The fraction of the world using LINUX

105

is only about 2%, which consists almost entirely of academics and a few government laboratories who don't know the word *customer*.

The Intel® compiler was free at one time, but now costs a bundle. Unless you're specifically developing applications for parallel processing there's no point, especially when other compilers are available for free. The optimization features that come with the Intel® compiler are useful, but nothing can come close to Walter Bright's -gt!

Appendix B. Reading Data with Flexibility

Built-in flexibility can make your applications stand out among the rest and inspire others in the workplace to seek you out when they need a new tool. An example of this is being able to read data in free format. Too many applications require data to be separated by one space but not two or more, to be comma separated, or to be tab-delimited. You can easily build your application to accept any of the above in any order, as illustrated by the following code:

```
n=0;
while(fgets(bufr,sizeof(bufr),fp))
    if(sscanf(bufr,"%lf%*[ ,\t]%lf%*[ ,\t]%lf",
        &X,&Y,&Z)==3)
        n++;
```

This reads from a file (using pointer fp), filling the buffer (bufr), scanning for values (X, Y, and Z), counting the trios (n++). The first directive of the string scanf (%lf) reads one double-precision floating-point value into the address of X (&X). The second directive (%*[,\t]) begins with percent (%) which means "scan a value" but is followed by an asterisk (*), which means discard the value. This directive continues with [,\t] (space comma tab). The square brackets ([]) work like regular expressions (an editing wonder not present in anything ever sold by Microsoft®). Combined %*[,\t] means scan anything that contains a space, comma, or tab into a string but discard the results. The next directive is another %lf or double-precision floating-point value. This sscanf() statement will read three numbers separated by any combination of spaces, commas, and/or tabs.

Allocating Arrays to Receive Data

We often read such data into arrays. In the early days of FORTRAN, many programs contained statements like the following:

```
DIMENSION X(999),Y(999),Z(999)
```

because we didn't know how many there would be and arrays were static, not dynamic. This type of coding should have disappeared with the T-Rex. We now write:

```
double*X,*Y,*Z;
X=calloc(n,sizeof(double));
Y=calloc(n,sizeof(double));
Z=calloc(n,sizeof(double));
```

or

```
X=calloc(3*n,sizeof(double));
Y=X+n;
Z=Y+n;
```

We might read the number of points on the first line of a file or allocate 1000 at a time, increasing the arrays with each additional 1000 values, or read through counting the values, allocate memory, rewind, and read again.

107

Appendix C. Saving a MetaFile from the Clipboard to a File

While metafiles are referenced throughout Windows® documentation, there are some essential aspect either not covered or buried so deep that they are not apparent. The code below will fetch a *pixel* (picture) or *vector* (drawing) from the clipboard and write it to a file on the disk that can be opened by some tools. The important distinction of this process being: to preserve the stroke-by-stroke details, which are lost when creating a **BMP** or **GIF** or **JPG** or any other *picture* format file. A picture loses some detail whenever stretched or shrunk or squashed, which it not the case with a vector drawing. Take not of each step and the order in which you must make them. Also know that the *Aldus placeable* header is essential to non-Microsoft tools but is never discussed and not provided by the Windows operating system.

```
#pragma pack(2)
    typedef struct{
        DWORD dwKey;
        WORD  wHandle;
        WORD  wLeft;
        WORD  wTop;
        WORD  wRight;
        WORD  wBottom;
        WORD  wInch;
        DWORD dwReserved;
        WORD  wCheckSum;
        }METAFILEHEADER;
#pragma pack()
int main(int argc,char**argv,char**envp)
    {
    int iForm;
    BYTE*pBits;
    char*fname;
    WORD w,*wptr;
    DWORD dwSize;
    ENHMETAHEADER eH;
    FILE*hFile;
    HDC hDC;
    HGLOBAL hClip;
    METAFILEHEADER mH;
    printf("creating Placeable Meta File from"\
      " clipboard\n");
    printf("  checking clipboard availability\n");
    if(!IsClipboardFormatAvailable(CF_ENHMETAFILE))
        {
        printf("EMF not available\n");
        return(0);
        }
    printf("  opening clipboard\n");
    if(!OpenClipboard(NULL))
        {
```

```
    printf("can't open clipboard\n");
    return(0);
    }
printf("  getting clipboard data\n");
if((hClip=GetClipboardData(
    CF_ENHMETAFILE))==NULL)
    {
    printf("can't get clipboard data\n");
    return(0);
    }
printf("  initializing enhanced metafile header\n");
memset(&eH,0,sizeof(ENHMETAHEADER));
eH.nSize=sizeof(ENHMETAHEADER);
if(!GetEnhMetaFileHeader(hClip,
    sizeof(ENHMETAHEADER),&eH))
    {
    printf("can't get header\n");
    return(0);
    }
printf("  initializing Aldus header\n");
mH.dwKey=0x9AC6CDD7L;
mH.wTop=1000*eH.rclFrame.top/2540;
mH.wLeft=1000*eH.rclFrame.left/2540;
mH.wRight=1000*eH.rclFrame.right/2540;
mH.wBottom=1000*eH.rclFrame.bottom/2540;
printf("  frame: %li,%li,%li,%li\n",
    eH.rclFrame.top,eH.rclFrame.left,
    eH.rclFrame.right,eH.rclFrame.bottom);
mH.wInch=1000;
wptr=(WORD*)&mH;
for(w=0;w<10;w++)
    mH.wCheckSum^=wptr[w];
printf("  getting reference device context\n");
if((hDC=GetDC(NULL))==0)
    {
    printf("can't get device context\n");
    return(0);
    }
printf("  getting metafile size\n");
if((dwSize=GetWinMetaFileBits(hClip,0,NULL,
    MM_ANISOTROPIC,hDC))==0)
    {
    printf("can't get size of bits\n");
    return(0);
    }
printf("  allocating memory for metafile\n");
if((pBits=malloc(dwSize))==NULL)
    {
    printf("can't allocate memory\n");
    return(0);
```

```c
  }
printf("  getting metafile contents\n");
if(GetWinMetaFileBits(hClip,dwSize,pBits,
  MM_ANISOTROPIC,hDC)!=dwSize)
  {
  printf("can't get data bits\n");
  return(0);
  }
printf("  releasing reference device context\n");
ReleaseDC(NULL,hDC);
if(argc>1)
  fname=argv[1];
else
  fname="clip2wmf.wmf";
printf("  creating file: %s\n",fname);
if((hFile=fopen(fname,"wb"))==NULL)
  {
  printf("can't create file\n");
  return(0);
  }
printf("  writing header (%u bytes)\n",
  sizeof(METAFILEHEADER));
if(fwrite(&mH,1,sizeof(METAFILEHEADER),
  hFile)!=sizeof(METAFILEHEADER))
  {
  printf("can't write metafile header\n");
  return(0);
  }
printf("  writing data (%lu bytes)\n",dwSize);
if(fwrite(pBits,1,dwSize,hFile)!=dwSize)
  {
  printf("can't write metafile bits\n");
  return(0);
  }
printf("  closing file\n");
fclose(hFile);
printf("  releasing memory\n");
free(pBits);
printf("  closing clipboard\n");
if(!CloseClipboard())
  {
  printf("can't close clipboard\n");
  return(0);
  }
return(0);
}
```

111

Appendix D. Drawing Lines and Symbols

Drawing lines and symbols into a window (usually of type WS_STATIC) is relatively simple. For example, we draw a line using just two function calls:

```
int i,x[]={0,1,2,3...},y[]={4,5,6,...};
POINT p;
MoveToEx(hDC,x[0],y[0],&p);
for(i=1;i<sizeof(x)/sizeof(int);i++)
    LineTo(hDC,x[i],y[i]);
```

where hDC is the device context of the window. Usually, we need to calculate or at least scale the array of points (x,y) but that is easily done with a single call:

```
TextOut(hDC,x,y,text,strlen(text));
```

If the text must be positioned (e.g., centered horizontally or vertically) we can get the dimensions in the form of a SIZE object:

```
SIZE ts;
GetTextSize(hDC,text,strlen(text),&ts);
TextOut(hDC,x-ts.cx/2,y-ts.cy/2,text,strlen(text));
```

also by D. James Benton

3D Articulation: Using OpenGL, ISBN-9798596362480, Amazon, 2021 (book 3 in the 3D series).

3D Models in Motion Using OpenGL, ISBN-9798652987701, Amazon, 2020 (book 2 in the 3D series.

3D Rendering in Windows: How to display three-dimensional objects in Windows with and without OpenGL, ISBN-9781520339610, Amazon, 2016 (book 1 in the 3D series).

A Synergy of Short Stories: The whole may be greater than the sum of the parts, ISBN-9781520340319, Amazon, 2016.

Azeotropes: Behavior and Application, ISBN-9798609748997, Amazon, 2020.

bat-Elohim: Book 3 in the Little Star Trilogy, ISBN-9781686148682, Amazon, 2019.

Boilers: Performance and Testing, ISBN: 9798789062517, Amazon 2021.

Combined 3D Rendering Series: 3D Rendering in Windows®, 3D Models in Motion, and 3D Articulation, ISBN-9798484417032, Amazon, 2021.

Complex Variables: Practical Applications, ISBN-9781794250437, Amazon, 2019.

Compression & Encryption: Algorithms & Software, ISBN-9781081008826, Amazon, 2019.

Computational Fluid Dynamics: an Overview of Methods, ISBN-9781672393775, Amazon, 2019.

Computer Simulation of Power Systems: Programming Strategies and Practical Examples, ISBN-9781696218184, Amazon, 2019.

Contaminant Transport: A Numerical Approach, ISBN-9798461733216, Amazon, 2021.

CPUnleashed! Tapping Processor Speed, ISBN-9798421420361, Amazon, 2022.

Curve-Fitting: The Science and Art of Approximation, ISBN-9781520339542, Amazon, 2016.

Death by Tie: It was the best of ties. It was the worst of ties. It's what got him killed., ISBN-9798398745931, Amazon, 2023.

Differential Equations: Numerical Methods for Solving, ISBN-9781983004162, Amazon, 2018.

Equations of State: A Graphical Comparison, ISBN-9798843139520, Amazon, 2022.

Evaporative Cooling: The Science of Beating the Heat, ISBN-9781520913346, Amazon, 2017.

Forecasting: Extrapolation and Projection, ISBN-9798394019494, Amazon 2023.

Heat Engines: Thermodynamics, Cycles, & Performance Curves, ISBN-9798486886836, Amazon, 2021.

Heat Exchangers: Performance Prediction & Evaluation, ISBN-9781973589327, Amazon, 2017.

Heat Recovery Steam Generators: Thermal Design and Testing, ISBN-9781691029365, Amazon, 2019.

Heat Transfer: Heat Exchangers, Heat Recovery Steam Generators, & Cooling Towers, ISBN-9798487417831, Amazon, 2021.

Heat Transfer Examples: Practical Problems Solved, ISBN-9798390610763, Amazon, 2023.

The Kick-Start Murders: Visualize revenge, ISBN-9798759083375, Amazon, 2021.

Jamie2: Innocence is easily lost and cannot be restored, ISBN-9781520339375, Amazon, 2016-18.

Kyle Cooper Mysteries: Kick Start, Monte Carlo, and Waterfront Murders, ISBN-9798829365943, Amazon, 2022.

The Last Seraph: Sequel to Little Star, ISBN-9781726802253, Amazon, 2018.

Little Star: God doesn't do things the way we expect Him to. He's better than that! ISBN-9781520338903, Amazon, 2015-17.

Living Math: Seeing mathematics in every day life (and appreciating it more too), ISBN-9781520336992, Amazon, 2016.

Lost Cause: If only history could be changed..., ISBN-9781521173770, Amazon, 2017.

Mass Transfer: Diffusion & Convection, ISBN-9798702403106, Amazon, 2021.

Mill Town Destiny: The Hand of Providence brought them together to rescue the mill, the town, and each other, ISBN-9781520864679, Amazon, 2017.

Monte Carlo Murders: Who Killed Who and Why, ISBN-9798829341848, Amazon, 2022.

Monte Carlo Simulation: The Art of Random Process Characterization, ISBN-9781980577874, Amazon, 2018.

Nonlinear Equations: Numerical Methods for Solving, ISBN-9781717767318, Amazon, 2018.

Numerical Calculus: Differentiation and Integration, ISBN-9781980680901, Amazon, 2018.

Numerical Methods: Nonlinear Equations, Numerical Calculus, & Differential Equations, ISBN-9798486246845, Amazon, 2021.

Orthogonal Functions: The Many Uses of, ISBN-9781719876162, Amazon, 2018.

Overwhelming Evidence: A Pilgrimage, ISBN-9798515642211, Amazon, 2021.

Particle Tracking: Computational Strategies and Diverse Examples, ISBN-9781692512651, Amazon, 2019.

Plumes: Delineation & Transport, ISBN-9781702292771, Amazon, 2019.

Power Plant Performance Curves: for Testing and Dispatch, ISBN-9798640192698, Amazon, 2020.

Practical Linear Algebra: Principles & Software, ISBN-9798860910584, Amazon, 2023.

Props, Fans, & Pumps: Design & Performance, ISBN-9798645391195, Amazon, 2020.

Remediation: Contaminant Transport, Particle Tracking, & Plumes, ISBN-9798485651190, Amazon, 2021.

ROFL: Rolling on the Floor Laughing, ISBN-9781973300007, Amazon, 2017.

Seminole Rain: You don't choose destiny. It chooses you, ISBN-9798668502196, Amazon, 2020.

Septillionth: 1 in 10^{24}, ISBN-9798410762472, Amazon, 2022.

Software Recipes: Proven Tools, ISBN-9798815229556, Amazon, 2022.

Steam 2020: to 150 GPa and 6000 K, ISBN-9798634643830, Amazon, 2020.

Thermochemical Reactions: Numerical Solutions, ISBN-9781073417872, Amazon, 2019.

Thermodynamic and Transport Properties of Fluids, ISBN-9781092120845, Amazon, 2019.

Thermodynamic Cycles: Effective Modeling Strategies for Software Development, ISBN-9781070934372, Amazon, 2019.

Thermodynamics - Theory & Practice: The science of energy and power, ISBN-9781520339795, Amazon, 2016.

Version-Independent Programming: Code Development Guidelines for the Windows® Operating System, ISBN-9781520339146, Amazon, 2016.

The Waterfront Murders: As you sow, so shall you reap, ISBN-9798611314500, Amazon, 2020.

Weather Data: Where To Get It and How To Process It, ISBN-9798868037894, Amazon, 2023.

www.ingramcontent.com/pod-product-compliance
Lightning Source LLC
LaVergne TN
LVHW051737050326
832903LV00023B/966